To Dr. Daniel D. Williams—

Because in attitude of
mind and spirit I
want to feel related.

Sophia Lyon Fahs

January 13, 1965

*Worshipping Together*
*With Questioning Minds*

BU
1522
.F3
1965

Gift

8-1-74

84558

# Worshipping Together

# With Questioning Minds

by Sophia Lyon Fahs

BEACON PRESS                    BOSTON

Copyright © 1965 by Beacon Press
All rights reserved
Published simultaneously in Canada by
S. J. Reginald Saunders and Co., Ltd., Toronto
Library of Congress catalogue card number: 65-12241
Printed in the United States of America

The author gratefully acknowledges permission to reprint passages from *The American Student Hymnal* (Fleming H. Revell Company, Westwood, N.J.); the *Friends Intelligencer; My Country and My People,* by Lin Yu-tang (The John Day Company, Inc., Publishers, New York, N.Y.); *Eternity Can Wait,* by Carl J. Nelson (The Hunter Press, Milford, N.H.); "The Hamlet of A. MacLeish," by Archibald MacLeish, in *Collected Poems* (Houghton Mifflin Company, Boston, Mass.); *Seven Sunday Mornings,* by Robert T. Weston (The First Unitarian Church, Louisville, Ky.).

# Preface and Acknowledgments

Such a book as this is clearly not the product of a single person's mind or experiences. It is rather one person's gathering together of some of the learnings gained from the thoughts and experiences of a number of unusual individuals, children as well as adults, with whom it has been the author's great privilege to associate, often in intimate and deep ways.

I have long been indebted to the adults and the children belonging to three unusual and vital experimental Sunday Schools in whose leadership I was privileged for some fifteen years to participate. The first was the experimental Sunday School at Teachers College, Columbia University; the second, the Union School of Religion under the direction of the Department of Religious Education at Union Theological Seminary, New York City; and the third was the Junior Department of the Church School of the Riverside Church of New York City. Fortunately, in all these Sunday Schools, weekly written reports in narrative form of work done and of experiences, both in the Services of Worship and in the classrooms, were required and kept on file.

About half of this book consists of selections from the reports, written during the nine years of my own leadership of the Junior Department in the Riverside Church School, together with a few other reports sent me by younger colleagues who since then have also been trying out fresh ideas and methods.

The other half of the book takes the form of chapters presenting my own reflections on such accumulated experiences, including questions and tentative proposals of a theological, philosophical, and educational nature. I have had especially in mind the hope of accenting and enriching the religious components in the overall processes of education by finding and calling attention to the essential interdependence of mind and heart, of reverence and inquiry.

In acknowledging my indebtedness, I shall go back to only a few of the Great Ones with whom I have been a contemporary and who taught me more than they will ever know. First, there were the professors: Frank McMurry, John Dewey, William Heard Kilpatrick, Goodwin Watson, and Ernest Osborne. There were also those with whom I was intimately associated in the field of Religious Education: Harrison S. Elliott; C. Ivar Hellstrom; and Harry Emerson Fosdick, the senior minister of the Riverside Church.

The teachers and colleagues with whom I worked intimately week after week in the church taught me more than I can ever say. Margaret Edwards, Emily Ellis, Mildred Tenny, Alice Cobb, Elsie Bush, Alice Owsley, and many more contributed continually to the richness of our program. I wish to mention also the learnings that came to us through our specialized leaders: Betty Fleming Smith, in creative dance; Evangeline Lewis, in creative drama; Max Exman, in creative music; and Eva Lewis Smith, our psychological adviser.

In addition, there are the friends who have loaned me the reports of their more recent experiments in other churches: Manzie T. Gill of the Methodist Church in Elma, New York; Ruth Koshuk, one-time leader of the Church School in the Northside Unitarian Church of Pittsburgh; William A. Shimer, then editor of *The American Scholar,* and a number of other experimentally-minded leaders whose reports I had hoped to include and could not because of lack of space.

I wish to name with a special sense of gratitude the two men whose poetical expressions I have chosen to use, with their permission, as two "theme songs" of the entire book: Lin Yu-tang and Howard Thurman. Added to these are two Unitarian ministers, Robert T. Weston of Omaha, Nebraska, and Carl J. Nelson of Eugene, Oregon, who granted me permission to use quotations from their writings.

In addition, I recall the scores of children whose honest, inquiring minds were a continual spur to my own thinking. Nor would I omit the four of our own children who lived long enough to ask questions, and my husband; all of whom, by their direct and loving honesty were continually opening doors for me into life.

I am especially indebted to my eldest daughter, Dorothy Fahs Beck, for her mature and discerning criticisms of this manuscript, and for her encouragement to me to persevere in the struggle to write it.

I wish to express also my thankfulness to Ernest W. Kuebler, past Director of the Division of Religious Education of the American Unitarian Association, to whom I owe the opportunity given me for twenty-five years to share in editing the curricular materials for the American Unitarian Association, and to Henry H. Cheetham, the present Director of the Department of Education of the Unitarian Universalist Association, for continuing that opportunity. I wish to express also my thankfulness for the encouragement given me by Dorothy T. Spoerl, the present editor of curricular materials, and Edward Darling of the Beacon Press.

Finally, I would add a word of thanks to all those

others who have given of their labor and thought toward putting the book into attractive printed form and for promoting its delivery to those who may care to read it.

Sophia Lyon Fahs, 1964

# Contents

*Worshipping Together*
*With Questioning Minds*

I will sing a new song.
I must learn the new song for the new needs.
I must fashion new words born of all the new growth of my
    life—of my mind—of my spirit.

I must prepare for new melodies that have never been mine
    before,
That all that is within me may lift my voice unto God.
Therefore, I shall rejoice with each new day
And delight my spirit in each fresh unfolding.

I will sing, this day, a new song unto the Lord.

Howard Thurman

# CHAPTER ONE

# A Falling Apart of Mind and Heart

"We are born too late for the old,
and too early for the new faith."

RALPH WALDO EMERSON [1]

We of the West live in a culture that is confused and inarticulate with regard to religion. We boast of our love of religious freedom, the right of each person to believe or not to believe in God in his own way, while at the same time we have been afraid to discuss our differing beliefs with one another, for we lack both the language and the background of knowledge needed for intelligent conversation.

The venerable and beautiful traditions to which we were educated are losing their hold on human belief, day by day . . . The old forms rattle and the new delay to appear . . . The mind, haughty with its sciences, disdains the religious forms as childish.

In consequence of this it appears as the misfortune of this period that the cultivated mind has not the happiness and dignity of the religious sentiment . . . We are born too late for the old, and too early for the new faith.[1]

These words spoken by Emerson, in 1879, to a gathering of students at the Harvard Divinity School seem surprisingly appropriate still. Our younger generation, as his, "haughty with its sciences, disdains the religious forms as childish." Some have been pushed

into atheism by their science studies; yet unconsciously
perhaps they may still feel emotionally bound by a nostalgia for the faith that once gave them comfort and
security. Others have rejected their parents' ethics and
religious ceremonials mainly because of their compulsive emotional need to feel freed from the belittling
restrictions of childhood and from the stigma of super-
stition. Both groups are ambivalent, feeling a sense of
loss, and yet glorying in their liberty. Both groups are
rebels and would feel it is "too late for the old," yet
some of them might still be persuaded to re-examine
religion if their emotions could be satisfied and their
minds partly appeased.

Among other members of our present society, rebellion against religion has been developing into two
distinctly different forms. One of these is an intellectual, outspoken rebellion against certain inherited religions, but not against religion as such. These rebels
are really hungry for something better than they have
yet found. This is evidenced by the phenomenal growth
of membership in outspoken liberal religious societies
such as the Unitarian Universalist Association. It is
evidenced also by the popularity of certain groups
that might be likened somewhat to "personality cults"
with a popular modern scientific flair. It is evidenced
also by the surprisingly successful efforts of Buddhist,
Hindu, and Moslem missionaries in America to make
converts.

In contrast to these religion-hungry groups today
are the large and growing number of persons who apparently have lost all interest in any religion. None
seems to be relevant in today's world as they see it.
They have pushed religion aside from the main streams
of life. Except as religion intrudes itself upon them on

certain public and formal occasions, and except as it sometimes seems needed by their growing children, they are ignoring religion altogether. They permit it to exist merely as a relic of man's primitive past. For both of these groups, the religion-hungry rebels and the wholly indifferent, it is indeed still too late for the old; yet for some it may not be too early for something new.

There is, however, still another common attitude toward religion which has developed widely since Emerson's time and that is in striking contrast to both of these. This is possibly the most powerful of the movements. At least it is the best organized and is most conscious of its purpose. This movement is being led by outstanding leaders in the dominant religious organizations of the West. It is evidenced by a united, well-organized, and well-financed effort to salvage as much of the old religious patterns of faith and practice, implied especially in the Christian religion, as can possibly be kept viable. This is being done by reforming the old ceremonies and dogmas here and there, and by reinterpreting history in so-called symbolic truths rather than in terms of realistic history, in order to retain the essentials of the Christian gospel as preached by the disciples of the first century. This movement is gathering strength in the form of one great ecumenical organization, the World Council of Churches, in order to save Christianity for the world. A strong evangelistic zeal to proclaim the Christian gospel as the one great hope of mankind is still evident in spite of the growing resistance in country after country to any such exclusive claims. For these it is not too late for the old in modified form. In fact, they are defending it vigorously.

## The Gathering Crisis

The striking differences between our present situation and that which characterized Emerson's day are to be found in the increased intensity of the gathering conflict, and in the world-wide spread of the signs of its approach.

Whereas in Emerson's day it seemed too early for the new, today the crisis is at hand. The serious issues can no longer be evaded if we are to avoid the "world-wide revolution" which Arnold Toynbee believes has already begun. He says that it is "taking place not merely on the political surface of life; this revolution is penetrating to the cultural and religious depths . . ." Then he adds his solemn prophecy: "And if this world-wide revolution is not to end in 'genocide' (and I for one do not expect that it will end that way), the only alternative possibility is that it will end in *a world-wide social fusion of all* tribes, nations, civilizations and *religions of Man*." [2] (Italics added.)

Is Dr. Toynbee a true prophet? Is the only alternative to a destructive revolution "the world-wide social fusion of all religions," along with the social fusion of "tribes, nations, and civilizations"? What would such a fusion actually imply? What kind of a fusion of religion might be worked out that would enhance religious feeling and make religion more relevant for life rather than speed the processes of disintegration now going on and increase the number of those who are indifferent? The crisis is impregnated with danger.

Such an alternative to destruction calls for a greatness of mind and heart, a vigorously honest and deep-delving scholarship, a greatly broadened outlook, the insights of profound wisdom, and the devoted fervor of creative thinkers. Where are such creative leaders to be found?

## The Specialized Issues Faced in This Book

Although it may seem fitting that I should apologize for beginning this book with such large generalizations regarding the world's religious predicament, I justify my so doing by the serious nature of the problems with which this book deals. In the concrete forms in which they appear here, they are indeed specialized, yet they are not problems for mere specialists to solve. They need to be examined within the framework of this world-wide religious crisis if they are to be understood.

The specialized issues faced in this book are those arising because the two parts of the usual Religious School session, namely, the so-called "services of worship" and the activities carried on within the separate classes seem to be drifting apart. Gathering the problems within a still smaller bundle, we shall have in mind primarily pre-adolescent children, from about nine to twelve or fifteen years of age. These services of worship in our liberal Religious Schools do not seem to be keeping pace with the inquiring, open, alert, exploring ways of thinking and doing going on in the classrooms.

## Why the Issue Is Especially Felt in Liberal Sunday Schools

Naturally this issue has been first felt in the more liberal Church Schools. As long as the class periods for study and the group gatherings for worship were both built on the assumption that the end sought was a loyal commitment to the specific religious faith of the particular church or synagogue involved, the two parts functioned naturally together; one part gave the children the knowledge and instruction needed to become followers of that religion, while the other part afforded the children an opportunity to express their loyalty in prayer and song, and for the adult leader to communicate an inspiration to continue in the faith.

Furthermore, most children's "services of worship" have been traditionally patterned after adult services. Many children have enjoyed these introductions into the adult world of formality and dignity, especially when they have been permitted to participate as leaders or ushers, or to sing in gowned choirs, and to join in the pageantry of processionals and recessionals.

Many adults who have shared such services with children have also found a sense of peace in the rhythmic beauty of the old litanies and Scripture readings and in the ordered steps of the ritual. Especially at the Easter and Christmas seasons, or during Passover and Hanukkah, many felt a nostalgia for the old melodies and ceremonies and myths, although the words and the symbols may have lost their intellectual appeal or perhaps the theologies expressed were never seriously contemplated.

On the other hand, some liberal religious leaders, more theologically conscious, can no longer find "happiness and dignity" in leading children in such expressions of religious sentiment. They themselves no longer feel honest in joining in the usual prayers, rituals, and songs of praise. They realize, too, that some of the children participating in them are doing little more than saying words, which are at some times vaguely understood and at others grossly misunderstood. Important and significant as symbols and ceremonies and beautiful words may be, these liberal leaders believe it is potentially dangerous to ask children to engage in ceremonies they do not understand or to use words that have no meaning for them. To do so week after week seems a denial of the potentialities of healthy childhood, a way of developing religious formalists and performers rather than personalities spontaneously free to be themselves and to think for themselves.

Impelled by a stern urge to be wholly honest, some of our liberal religious leaders, therefore, have ceased having "services of worship" in their Sunday Schools. They feel too agnostic to address prayers to "God the unknown." They feel obliged to be non-committal when the children ask about God, prayer, and worship. They would accept wholeheartedly John Bunyan's stern advice, "When thou prayest, rather let thy heart be without words, than thy words without a heart."

I speak with deep respect for those I am describing, for I have also often felt so inarticulate and uncertain that I have chosen silence. Yet the heart must not give up its need to find the words with which to express itself. There are appropriate times to be silent and there are times when words are needed. For me, learning how to lead services of worship with children has been a continuing struggle to find ways of being honestly articulate regarding my own religious philosophy of life. Learning to lead services of worship has required my own practicing of the questioning mind, intensifying my own observations of reality, expanding where possible my own conscious awareness of reality, increasing my own understandings. My companionship with children, and with leaders of children, in worshipping has been one of life's most blessed forms of experience.

I justify beginning with thoughts regarding the world-wide religious crisis, because of the serious problems involved. They are not merely questions of educational method or administration, such as whether children's meetings should be formal or informal; whether the leader should tell a story, give a sermonette, or lead a discussion; what should be the order of service; or which hymn book is best; etc. The problems with which this book deals, if seen in their dimensions of depth and breadth, are not problems for religious educators alone to consider. Nor are they merely children's problems to be understood by adults. The problems are in reality a reflection of prior problems in the lives of all of us, whether we are aware of them or not. We ourselves will be enriched both in mind and spirit if we consciously struggle with them.

Then, too, there is great need for many more leaders of high intellectual calibre, with informed interest and deep concern. As we have grown in understanding and in experience, we have developed in our liberal churches materials with which to implement such a philosophy as Toynbee has hinted at in his expression "the social fusion of all religions." From the very first steps with the youngest children, we have advocated accenting the universalized types of natural experiences most potent in awakening wondering awareness and reverent thinking, especially about invisible and intangible realities. During the following years of childhood, we have continued with this emphasis, enlarging the children's understanding of religious history so as to embrace differing religions, including the primary experiences of early men as well as those within the great, well-established religious cultures. We have hoped it would be possible to proceed so that the children would find ways to preserve the greater values in each religious perspective and to discard the weaknesses. We have hoped also that the children might develop an ability to empathize with any person who has sincerely conceived loyalties to his vision of what is good.

## Hopeful Intentions Within the Limits of This Book

So we return to the major issue with which we began and we shall examine it in its concrete setting. How can the spirit of inquiry, uncertainty, and wonder be brought into the larger meetings traditionally defined as "services of worship"? Most of us are not content simply to delete these general meetings from our programs. Nor are we satisfied in continuing to conduct them in a formal, traditional manner. To do the first would weaken the vitality of the more adventurous approach, and to do the other might even contradict the very values we have come to prize. How can questioning minds worship?

It is indeed "too late for the old," but it is no longer "too early for the new . . ."

# CHAPTER TWO

# Some Conditions for a New Unity

"Where is that unity of understanding to be found? To com-
bine real appreciation with critical appraisal, to see with the
mind and feel with the heart, to make the mind and heart one,
is no easy grace to attain to. . . . It requires courage, that rare
thing, honesty, and that still rarer thing, a constant questioning
activity of the mind."

LIN YU-TANG [1]

These discerning words of our contemporary Chinese philosopher, Dr. Lin Yu-tang, express the wistful
theme of this book. It is to achieve this "no easy grace
to attain to" with which we are concerned: appreciation
combined with critical appraisal; diversity gathered
within one purposeful fellowship; questioning what we
do not understand for the sake of commitment to what
we do understand.

As suggested in the first chapter, we may in a general way liken the studying in the separate classes of a
School of Religion to the mind's activities, and the experiences in the weekly gatherings for worship to those
of the heart. Just as the uninterrupted flow of fresh-
ened blood in and out of the brain is necessary to the
life of the entire physical body, so we may think of a
continuing interplay of communication between the
separate classes and the larger assemblies as essential to
the ongoing healthy life of any school. Surely one significant way in which to test the genuine vitality within

a school would be to note the nature of this interpenetration.

Changing the figure of speech, we may compare the
general assemblies of the school to "a common meeting
ground" where the children and leaders may bring their
special concerns and questions or their newly found
insights, and where in return they may receive the
enlivening thoughts of others.

Francis Parker, founder of the one-time famous
elementary school in Chicago where John Dewey as a
young man began his fruitful experimentation with his
life-giving theory of education, used to describe the
regular morning assemblies in his school as being like
"a family altar, to which each brings his offering . . .
the fruits of his observations and studies . . . where all
contribute and share the intellectual life of the school."

Such vital interpenetration between the varied
units within the school does not come about by mere
chance or of necessity. In fact, it is seldom achieved.
When it comes, it usually begins with one person, the
director of the school or the leader of the departmental
assemblies, who is himself thoroughly imbued with a
creative philosophy of education. The probability of
creating such an interplay between the classroom work
and the services of worship is enhanced when the leader
of the services of worship develops between himself and
the teachers a feeling of being comrades together in an
interesting and mutually trusting partnership, each
needing help from the others. The warmth of the
partnership grows also when the teachers learn how to
write honest and realistic narrative reports of each
weekly experience with the children and these reports
are read regularly by the leader of the departmental
services. If, in addition, the two can have conferences

together, not only for the sake of helping the teacher
but also for the sake of giving suggestions to the leader
of the services, the possibilities are greatly increased for
a vital interpenetration between classes and assemblies.

Such methods of planned mutual give and take, I
have found in my own experience to be essential. How
seldom, however, are these procedures followed; and
in how many situations they may seem wholly imprac-
tical! I can only hope that some such ideal may not be
wholly forgotten, and that at least some attempts to
achieve it partially will be made. Anything worth doing
is usually difficult, at least in the beginning. Yeast
requires time to spread its life. The process of growth
is hidden. On the other hand, nothing happens until
the yeast has been planted and unless it is itself alive.

This interpenetration of learned values between
the classroom work and the services of worship, however, involves more than changes in schedules and
activities. The yeasty elements in the changed philosophies that need planting are more subtle and hidden;
and hence more difficult to discover and assimilate. I
can merely suggest several largely untraveled directions
in which I believe we must move.

1. As leaders we need to strive for a deeper understanding of the *motives and emotional biases* that the
children bring with them into their study of religion.
Where are their real interests pointing? Why do they
come to Sunday School? What is it they think they are
studying? Does "religion" seem relevant to their living
or is it some vague burden that was imposed upon them
when younger, without their consent or understanding
and from which they would now like to escape?

In short, a primary need for both leaders and children *is to find a truly strong motive for coming together*

*once a week to study religion.* It is not merely the parents and teachers who need to feel that the children should study religion and morality. It is the children themselves, and the children alone, who can supply the really satisfactory motivation.

During the first few weeks of any given year, the leader of the departmental services has a peculiar opportunity to awaken in children vitalizing motives for studying religion. This can be done in a variety of ways. Samples of some of the ways we ourselves have tried can be found in the illustrations which follow this chapter. Sometimes it was done by encouraging the children to recall some of their own personal unforgettable experiences, which they may not have labeled as religious although they engendered deeper or more expansive feelings, emotions, and thoughts than usual. Sometimes it was done by the leader's telling a suggestive story. At other times we encouraged each child to think over the questions that he would most like to have answered and pick out the one that he would like to have answered more than any other. When such questions were brought out, and we looked at them together, we found that they were very much like the questions that people everywhere have been asking and that religious leaders have tried to answer by assuming some religious belief. Thus we introduced religion as being man's thoughts and feelings about such questions as they themselves had asked.

We tried to let the children know that, in such a school of religion as ours, they should feel free to ask any kind of question they seriously wanted answered. We would not promise to answer their questions; but we would promise to join them in trying to find some of the answers men have given. We found that such approaches as these awakened the children's interest, thus engendering motives for studying and experiencing religion for themselves.

2. This observation leads us to direct our attention to another element in a creative educational and religious philosophy that, if lived with and emphasized, would involve marked changes in the usual assumptions regarding the development of reverent and worshipful attitudes of mind. This is *the need to learn how to lead children to face the issues of life in direct and realistic ways.*

Such *a philosophy of realism* leads to a desire that the whole of any given situation be examined, and that the issues be seen from the points of view of the several persons involved. It means also that different possible solutions should be imagined, possibly several of these experimented with, and that the solution finally chosen be decided on the basis of all these factors. Children need opportunities to discover in their own experiencing how our lives are intertwined, and so to have their imaginations enlarged and their empathies deepened.

Although such realism seems complicated when analyzed in this way, the learning can be done in very concrete steps when the situation is actually experienced by the child or adult. Even kindergarten children are learning to make their own decisions in play in this thoughtful and sensitive manner. It is the most natural way of learning how to live together that can be conceived. In fact, surprising as it may seem, it was in the kindergartens of the country that this realistic and sensitive dealing with immediate problems was first tried out and found to be creatively fruitful.

As teachers of older children also have grown in their understanding of the real import of this realistic *learning in experience,* classroom activities have become more natural. There are fewer admonitions to be unselfish, fewer rebukes for badness, fewer external rewards and punishments, and more imaginative suggestions given to lead children to watch the reactions of others and to identify in feeling with them.

Although in the children's assemblies there are not such opportunities for informal fellowship, in which to experiment and to learn, as in a single classroom, actual experiences can be vividly recalled and examined in these general assemblies, sometimes with even more poise and freedom than when one is in the very midst of heated emotional experiences. Stories also can be vividly told, about other children or about adults, those from the past or those who are contemporaries. These can be experienced in imagination, by hearing their stories told, not to teach moral lessons but to portray problematic situations where there were several possible solutions and a choice had to be made between what was more desirable and what was less so, neither being ideal.

Such an educational philosophy need not in the end destroy or even lessen the children's idealism. It does, however, require revision in time-honored ways of facing the moral issues of life. Morality has been taught for so long mainly through the promulgation of laws and the teaching of general principles to live by, that today there are still many who are unable even to call a problem a "moral" one unless some rule can be made regarding how it should be solved or by which one can determine clearly between the way that is right and the other that is wrong. If there are several possible solutions it is commonly said that the problem is no longer a "moral" issue; it is simply a personal one.

A realistic philosophy, however, brings all inter-personal problems into the moral realm. In fact, the more complicated the situation and the more difficult it is to decide on the best or "the right" solution, the greater becomes one's moral responsibility and the greater the need to increase understanding and to en-large sympathies before making a decision between what is better and what may be less desirable in view of all the persons and conditions involved. Although, as a result, our ethics are called "relative," by so doing *we* become more understanding, more sensitive emo-tionally, and more able to feel empathy toward others.

3. In the third place, this realistic examination of the issues of life in this age of emphasis upon the sci-ences, encourages and even requires *a broadening of the realm of man's religious and ethical responsibility until it includes his relations with all forms of Reality. It includes our ethical responsibility to Nature,* con-ceived broadly as including all forms of life as well as all that is inanimate, all forms of intangible energies and tangible matter, both psychological experiences and physical conditions.

The Judaeo-Christian Bible long ago assumed a vital link between Deity and Nature. Yet with man-kind's changed understandings of Nature, the Western world has not been able to accept the full implications of this scientific revolution by changing its religious beliefs accordingly. The tendency has been rather to retreat, as it were, to the Scriptures and to religious traditions rather than to face realistically "the Book of Nature" and read its messages as an important part of what Thomas Paine called "the Word of God."

*The modern sciences support a realistic naturalism in religion.* During the past fifty years scientists have been continually disclosing deeper and more extensive levels of energy in immeasurably gigantic and unnumbered galaxies, with matter and energy as two forms of one essence, with body and spirit apparently interwoven and inseparable, with time merging into eternity, till the human spirit is awed in reverence beyond all expression.

Although the areas of man's knowledge have grown by leaps and bounds, unexplored mysteries still fill every nucleus of every atom in every living or dead body, every planet and star, and all the far-reaching stretches of outer space millions of light years away. As more and more of the hidden energies within the natural universe are discovered, the more awe-inspiring become its diversities within its unity, its disorder within its order, its creative and living potentials within its abiding designs. Although superficial men may sometimes become "haughty with their sciences," yet in their greater and more sensitive moments most scientists are deeply moved by an unspeakable reverence.

Increasing evidence is being found to justify the postulate that there was, and is, and is to come a creating, evolving, designing, unifying, all-enveloping *Life, Mind, Spirit, Mysterium Tremendum* to whom the word "God" may be appropriately given.

We have come to this conclusion because of what we think has been discovered by scientists, our own personal intuitive experiences, our historical inheritances, and through faith. There is a modicum of uncertainty in our belief, yet we live with this hope and shall continue to act as if it were true until the evidence of fresh knowledge or of personal experience calls for a revision. We intend to keep on questioning, watching, experiencing, and expecting richer understanding.

My experience tells me that we live in a century when religion, if it is to survive, must become more realistic within the natural world than it has been in the past. Mankind today is so overwhelmed by his awareness of the vastness and power within natural time and natural space that he has lost some of that yearning to look beyond into eternity or up into a realm beyond the natural.

This changed philosophy that I believe is slowly developing in our time, and that may help us to become more integrated persons again, is not only *a realistic humanism*. It is also *a realistic naturalism*. To assimilate it truly, involves large changes in our ways of study and worship; not only what we study, but how we study; not only whom we worship, but even why we are reverent.

It may even be called *a realistic natural theism;* but it cannot be equated simply with a belief in one God, nor with a belief in an intellectual abstraction. It is more than words can describe. It is a feeling of being a part of a Universal Living Unity.

4. A reverent asking of questions of Reality (conceived in this broad and realistically living way) can appropriately be called a way of praying. The six days and nights that George Washington Carver spent in his Tuskegee laboratory asking questions of the peanut were in reality spent in prayer.* Sir Isaac Newton's hours of questioning why the apple fell and the moon did not by means of which he learned of the law of gravity, were in essence spent in prayer.

The personal exhilaration of feeling a part of a living chain reaching into the past and into the future, of

* See the four stories about George Washington Carver in the Illustrations from Experience for Chapter Three.

being a link between what is here and what is everywhere—this is an experience that I have learned to
hope for and to expect some children to experience
when I realistically and seriously delve with them into
some specific bit of Reality.

As long as I live I do not expect to forget that
morning during one of our Junior Department services
of worship when I had vivid evidence that some of the
boys and girls, at least, felt an exhilaration in their
realization of being linked with the ages. We had been
discussing how old we were and when we really began.
We traveled in imagination step by step back from our
own birthdays to the time of our conception, then on
to our parents' birthdays, and to our grandparents', and
our great grandparents' and so on, and on. We decided
finally that something now within our bodies must have
been living hundreds, thousands, millions of years ago.
We could never get back to our own beginnings. We
must then all be very, very, very old; or at least something within us must be billions of years old.

The experience was a thrilling one for me, but I
had not expected to find it had been even more thrilling
to some of the children. I learned later that, after the
service was over, a group of boys in one class ran down
the stairs to their classroom in order to greet their
teacher when she arrived later, with the gleeful declara-
tion "Hurrah! we are as old as you are! We are as old
as you are!"

Such experiences may not come often, yet they are
beyond price when they are experienced. Nor are they
usually generated in children's groups through some
generalized talk about the universe. Such experiences
arise more often when some simple concrete meditation
in questioning one thing or one event is elicited.

In some of our church schools it has become almost a habit for the leader of the services of worship to have some natural object, or objects, on an altar or table in the chancel or on the platform where it may become the center of attention and awaken curiosity. Perhaps the object is a branch of autumn leaves, a rose or lily, a flowering plant, an unusual stone, or a bowl of apples or oranges. Sometimes each boy and girl on entering the room is given a small object to hold in his hands, such as a bean, a seed, a leaf, a flower.

Sermonizing through object lessons for children is no newly-discovered art. It has long been known that an object that can be seen is highly successful as a device to awaken children's interests; and that from the visible, one can direct attention to the invisible.

If, however, we truly believe in a religion nurtured in realistic natural experiences rather than in visions of supernatural events, we have a different reason for starting by asking questions of things that boys and girls can see or handle. Rather than using things in order to find spiritual lessons from them, we consider things in order to discover more of their own true nature. In the terminology of today's philosophers, we would say, in order to know them "existentially."

Wendell and Jimmie in our sixth-grade class could have helped me lead a service of worship, had I been sensitive enough at the time to see the possibilities. For one day in class Wendell had said, "Some one says that if you boiled all the chemicals in your body down and sold them, they'd be worth only seven cents. It's the way you're put together that's the hard part." And Jimmie had added: "just chemicals can't have children."

We might have filled a table with containers holding samples of the different chemical elements in one human body. What dynamic questions might have been awakened! How reverently we would have felt as together we stood before the Great Mystery of Life!

We need not labor to reach up into another realm to feel the touch of Infinity. Although it is far off, yet it is also nearer than hands or feet. We can never know anything, even the most microscopic bit of matter or protoplasm, without facing what eludes our understanding and even our imagination. As Rufus Jones once said, "There is a more yet in our very being." There is a "more yet" in every being, in every thing. It is really not strange that what mankind has believed is in a "supernatural" realm can already be here in the natural.

"Consider the lilies of the field, how they grow . . ." said Jesus. "Consider the flower in the crannied wall," said Tennyson.

"Consider anything you please," says the Zen Buddhist, "But just consider it not as a symbol of eternity, as God in miniature, as a moral lesson or as a Great White Hope, but just consider it." [2]

By the way of summary, let us rethink the four needed revisions in our personal attitudes and philosophies that have been suggested if, in our generation, we can hope to keep our minds and hearts working in harmony together. First is the greater emphasis we need to put on understanding inner feelings, especially motivations and unconscious assumptions. Second is the significance of learning to face life's issues realistically and understandingly. Third is the need not only for *a natural humanism,* but also for *a religious naturalism* that brings the whole of Nature into the area of ethical concern and religious appreciation. And finally the need to question concrete bits of Reality until we feel the nearness of the Universal. Other equally important changes may have been omitted. These here considered, however, are worthy of much meditation and will require persistent learning in actual experiencing.

We are left with a feeling of the greatness of our unknowing, and with the need for a continuing questioning attitude of mind. This, so significant a thought, we shall consider in our next chapter.

## Illustrations from Experience

*Visible and Invisible Realities*
*(First Sessions of a Summer School)*

A group of fifth and sixth grade boys and girls were gathered on a summer's day for the first session of a summer school. Sitting in a large circle, we told names, hobbies, whatever each wished to share. All shared quite freely. After this getting acquainted period, the question was raised regarding what the group might do.

JOE. Are we going to study about the same things we do in Sunday School?

LEADER. Would you like to?

JOE. No and yes.

LEADER. Tell us about your *no* and *yes*.

JOE. [*Apologetically.*] Well, what we study is all right, but there are some things we never get to. Why doesn't someone tell us who God really is, or don't they know?

SUSIE. And where He is. How can He be everywhere at the same time?

LEADER. We are asking some very important questions. Let's put them on the board where we can see and think about them a bit, and perhaps there are more questions.

CHILD. I want to know why the minister always says, "God is Spirit."

ANOTHER CHILD. Some people say, "He is inside of us."

LEADER. These are big questions, aren't they, the kind that many people for many years have puzzled over. Suppose we leave your questions on the board a few moments. I am going to ask you some. Maybe you will think my questions are something like a game. Whatever I mention, tell me whether it is something you can see or cannot see, visible or invisible. (Leader then mentions slowly words like trees, telephone pole, wind, —"Yes, we can see what it does, but not wind itself."— desk, love,—"Can you bring me a basketful?"—electric light, electric energy, atomic energy, courage, fear, a thought, thoughtfulness.)

LEADER. Let us go back and talk about the invisible things. Are they real? How do you know? Now one more game. Karen, tell me, where are you?

KAREN. [*All laughing.*] Why, I am right here.

LEADER. But I can't quite see you.

DOUG. This is some kind of a joke.

LEADER. No, really even though I am looking at Karen I find it difficult to see *her*. I can see her blue sweater, her blue eyes, a nice sun tan, a smile, but I still can not really see *her*.

DAVE. You're just kidding, or maybe it's some kind of a riddle.

ERIC. It is a riddle and I think I know the answer.

LEADER. Don't tell yet, Eric. Has anyone else discovered the answer to the riddle?

JOE. You mean you can't see her—her thoughts, what's going on in her mind?

SUSIE. Or maybe anything else, like things she doesn't want to tell, or like she would pray about.

LEADER. Yes, all these things are the part of Karen, or of any of you, that I cannot see. When Karen, or anyone of you smiles, I begin to see or feel your happiness, and when Eric raised his hand and said, "I think I know the answer to the riddle," I felt a bit of Eric's thoughts coming out to meet mine, even though he didn't answer the riddle in actual words. Let's go back for a moment to our visibles and invisibles.

[*We named them again, and then asked, "Where shall we put ourselves? Are we visible or invisible?" A chorus of "Both."* ]

NANCY. We're visible and we're invisible too.

LEADER. When we talked of the visible and invisible things, we agreed that the invisible things, energy, love, a thought, all these were as real as the visible things. What about ourselves, our thinking, loving, courageous, or fearful selves? Are they really real, too, as much as the part of you I am looking at?

ERIC. Of course, that's what is really us.

LEADER. Eric has put it very well. It's these thinking parts and these feeling parts, our very *aliveness,* that are really us. People call these invisible parts our *spirits.* God is spirit, and we, too, are spirit.

SUSIE. But we couldn't be everywhere at once like God.

LEADER. Couldn't we?

[*There was a chorus of "No!" "Hardly!" and "Unless you mean on television."*]

LEADER. Close your eyes for a few moments, everyone. Keep them closed until I tell you when you may
open them. (Speaking quietly and slowly) You are now
at home. You have just come there from school. The
minute you step in the door you smell something delicious. It smells like cookies baking. Perhaps they are
chocolate chip cookies. You hurry to the kitchen. "Oh,
Mother, I'm so hungry, may I have one right now?
What kind are they?"

Then Mother answers, "Yes, but they are still in
the oven. Run upstairs and change your clothes, and
then I think they will be ready." You become hungrier
and hungrier. Sure enough, they are ready. Mother
puts one in your hand saying, "Careful, they are still a
little hot." How luscious, just full of chocolate chips,
and Mother says that you may have two more right now.

Now open your eyes. How many of us were right
there at home eating those cookies?

EVERYONE. I was, I was. I could even taste them.
Oh, please, Mrs. Gill, don't do that to us again. I can't
stand it. It was so real to me I almost forgot where I
was.

LEADER. Well, where were you, at home or here?

DOUGLAS. We were here, but you could say we
weren't all here, that is, our thoughts were home.

JOE. So were our taste buds!

ERIC. I think I was almost more home than I was
here.

LEADER. Do you think then that it is possible for
you to be in two places at the same time?

SUSIE. Yes, I know it is.

LEADER. God is spirit, and we are spirit. We are
not going to talk any more right now. We are going to
sit here together quietly, and go over in our minds the

questions and answers that have come to us this morning.

Before we separated, I suggested that they take time again before the day was over to be quiet. "Perhaps out of doors all by yourself, somewhere," I said. "Think over again what we have talked about. Think of the many different places you can be without your visible body going anywhere. Take time to feel your own spirit. God, too, is spirit. We are like God. Next time we meet we can talk together longer."

Next morning we met outdoors in a quiet secluded spot, to continue our thinking. Our discussion centered about the different ways in which things are seen and heard. We made believe we were insects walking through the grass, and tried to think how a small twig, small stones, or blades of grass would appear to such an ant-person. (Several magnifying glasses helped us at this point.)

JOE. What would things look like if we were supermen, or giants?

KAREN. Probably just like they do from an airplane.

DOUG. Yes, the rivers look like tiny brooks, and the cities look like my brother's building blocks.

SUSIE. The cars look like little toy cars, or if you get high enough they almost look like a procession of insects moving along a tiny thread. And the people, well, they are just ants or maybe viruses that you couldn't even see.

LEADER. Suppose you took your insect eyes with you on the airplane?

[*There was a burst of laughter at this.*]

JOE. You wouldn't even know there was anything

to look for or see except maybe the man's foot you were next to.

LEADER. [*After considerable discussion.*] Let us try turning our ears to hear things outdoors that we would not ordinarily hear. Scientists tell us that the woods are full of nature noises or sounds deep down in the moss, in the roots, in the leaves of the trees, sounds that the human ear seldom or never hears.

ERIC. [*After frantically waving his hand.*] I think I know where we are going.

LEADER. Explain what you mean, Eric.

ERIC. Well, I think it's something like this. All we've said in class today is really the same thing we talked about yesterday—visible and invisible things and our real selves. You might say we've got sort of an inner eye that helps us understand things our ordinary eyes don't. You could even call it a spiritual eye if you wanted to.

[*Eric's insight brought the whole class a "that's it" feeling. In the wordless moments that followed our inner eyes were seeing things.*]

LEADER. Many years ago another person thinking deeply like ourselves felt as we feel right now, and he spoke very much as Eric has today. This is what he said:

"What no eye has ever seen,
what no ear has ever heard,
what never entered the mind of man,
God has prepared all that for those who love him.
And God has revealed it to us by the Spirit, for the Spirit fathoms everything, even the depths of God.
What human being can understand the thoughts of a
man,

except the man's own inner spirit?
So too no one understands the thoughts of God,
except the Spirit of God."

I Cor. 2:9-11 *Moffatt Translation*

JOE. I guess we could say that we were built for a visible world and an invisible world. If we used our invisible eyes more we might answer our own questions. I begin to think we really could.

[*This experience has been reported by Mrs. Manzie T. Gill, Elma, New York.*]

### *When We Shared Some Unforgettable Experiences*

### Talk by Leader

This first Sunday of our new year is something like a birthday for all of us together. For some it is a fourth beginning; for some it may be a sixth; for some it may be a first. (I called for hands to show the children who had been coming to the school ever since they were in Nursery School, those who began in the Primary Department, and those who were new this year. I was especially interested to learn that so many had been coming for a number of years.)

For all of us this is a special day because we are beginning a new year. We are like travelers going into a new country, who wonder what they are going to see and what they are going to do. We look ahead at the weeks before us and ask, "Are we going to like this new year? Are we going to discover anything we do not already know? What would we like to find out about?"

But let us get better acquainted with one another first. Sometimes at this service I shall tell you a story. This morning I am going to ask you to tell stories, little ones about yourselves. I want you to think back over this past summer and try to remember some one time when something happened to you, or when you did something, or you saw something, that made you stop and wonder more than usual about things. Some time when you felt your thoughts stretching out and out after something that you had never thought of before. Perhaps it was a time when you felt very full of feelings. Perhaps you never have put them into words, or you never told anybody about them. Perhaps it was a time when you began thinking about God all by yourself without anyone reminding you that it was time to say your prayers.

Such moments are not easy to tell about, but I hope that you will not be timid because I think we will feel closer together and better acquainted if we can tell these things to one another.

I have asked the pianist to play softly for a few moments while we collect our thoughts. (I then suggested that the children who wished to tell something stand and wait their turn to speak. Almost immediately six or ten children were on their feet.) The following are some of the things which they said as well as I can remember them:

BOY. I was in Sequoia Park this summer and saw those great big trees. They seemed so wonderful. It was all dark around, and yet it was not dark.

GIRL. I found a bird this summer that had hurt its foot, and I brought it into the house and took care of it. When it was well, I let it fly away. One day later I saw this very bird being killed by a hawk. It made me feel all funny inside.

BOY. A few weeks ago I saw the Aurora Borealis. It seemed very wonderful. There were lots of colors: green and white and pink.

BOY. [*Scarcely waiting for the other boy to finish.*] I saw it, too, out in the country. Mother said it looked like a sunset and a sunrise all at once. As I watched, I was sort of scared and amazed too.

BOY. The other day I was on the street and saw a big crowd, and I thought it must be an accident. But I found out that there was a blind man trying to cross the street and another man was helping him. I thought here was a guy who helps other people when they need him, and I thought it was up to us guys to help other guys who cannot help themselves.

GIRL. I was up in Vermont. I climbed a high mountain. I could look down on the country all around and could see so much sky and clouds. It made me feel grand and sort of free.

BOY. I was riding with my father in the car at night. In the light of the headlights we saw a skunk in the road. It was the first time I had ever seen a skunk. [*This remark caused a little snickering, and another child told of having seen a dead skunk on the road.*]

GIRL. One day this summer I got angry with my little sister. I hit her, and she hit me back. So Mother sent me up to my room and shut the door, and I cried. Then I decided to pray to God and ask him to help me be kind to my sister so I would not hit her any more.

BOY. I was riding in a car this summer, and suddenly we saw a deer jumping over the fence. He ran away into the woods.

GIRL. I was walking down the path with our Great

Dane. All of a sudden a beautiful deer ran right out in front of us. I felt a funny feeling inside.

BOY. I stepped out of our house at night and saw a wild animal moving around in the bushes and I began to think of all the animals in the woods at night and wondered what they were doing.

Since the time for closing the service had about come, we stopped telling our stories and the leader tried to express the children's thoughts and feelings in a prayerful form:

LEADER. We are thankful that such unforgettable moments can come to us. May we keep our minds awake and watchful so that we may have them more often. It has been good to remember them and to talk them over together. Amen.

### A Boy Who Had Never Heard of God

(This story was told in one of the earliest meetings of the school year.) Can any of you remember back to the time when your mother or father first spoke to you about God, or when you first heard someone else speak of God? (One child only in the group responded in the affirmative. The others seemed unable to think back far enough to remember a time before they had ever heard God mentioned.) Suppose you had grown to be as old as you are now and no one had ever mentioned God to you, or you had never gone to church, or had never been taught to pray. Do you think that all by yourself you would have come to the conclusion that there must be someone or something like God? (No answer.)

I am going to tell a true story of a boy named Wilhelm who lived to be ten years old before he ever heard anyone speak of God. Wilhelm lived in Germany about one hundred years ago. His mother had died when he was only three, so that he and his father were left to live together alone. But his father was a very wonderful father as you shall see.

Shortly after the mother's death, the father decided to move out into the country with his son and to live on a farm where there were no neighbors to talk with. Of course, Wilhelm was often lonely for his mother, but he was quite happy because his father was an interesting companion and Wilhelm was devoted to him. On a farm there are always many things to do, and there is much to see. Wilhelm's playmates were the cats and the dogs, the chickens and the geese, the horses, and the cows.

When Wilhelm grew old enough to be sent to school the father decided that he would teach his son himself. He and Wilhelm, therefore, had their own school each day. When the weather was warm and pleasant they usually met outdoors where there were always many things to find out about. The father thought these things were as important for Wilhelm to learn as for him to learn to read books. So the father taught his boy as they fed the baby kittens, or as they played with the new puppies. Besides, there were many interesting things to learn about the geese and the chickens and the birds. As Wilhelm tried to help his father plant or weed the garden, he always had questions to ask about

this vegetable or that flower. Sometimes the two had
their school while they strolled together slowly through
the woods, hunting for wild flowers and snails and little
animals.

As Wilhelm grew older and could carry more responsibility, he learned to ride a horse and to milk the
cows. During the winter evenings, his father taught
him to carve in wood the shapes of things and animals.
Wilhelm thought his father a very wonderful person because he knew so much and was able to do so many hard
things.

As the days passed and Wilhelm grew older, he
began to wonder about some things. His father's
answers didn't satisfy him. His father could do a great
many things, but there were still left many things
which nobody seemed able to do.

There was the rain, for example. One day Wilhelm
wanted his father to make it rain. The garden needed it
badly, but his father said he couldn't do it. Another day
Wilhelm wanted his father to make the wind stop blowing so hard, and his father said he couldn't do it. And
again, Wilhelm wanted his father to make a dead baby
chicken wake up and walk, but his father said nobody
could make anything with life in it.

These things puzzled Wilhelm. Who did these
things then? His father didn't seem interested to help
him answer his questions. So Wilhelm had to work out
an answer all his own. He finally decided that it was
the Sun up in the sky that did all these things that
nobody else could do. Even when it was dark he
thought the Sun could do things. Wilhelm liked to
think about the Sun and all the things it could do, and
sometimes when he was alone he felt like talking to the
Sun. It was a long way off, he knew, but still it seemed

near. The Sun seemed to Wilhelm like a wonderful and strong friend. Wilhelm did feel lonely sometimes for a friend, someone else besides his father. He wished he had at least a mother. It was comforting to feel that the good Sun was up there in the sky. But all these thoughts Wilhelm kept secret.

Then one morning, waking early before it was light, Wilhelm dressed in the dark and stepped quietly downstairs and out of doors all by himself. The Sun was still hiding behind the hills beyond the valley at the side of the house. Wilhelm stood for a while alone, looking out at the eastern sky. He watched the fleecy clouds turn slowly pink and then golden with light. When finally the bright golden ball peeped above the hilltops, it seemed to Wilhelm like a great Lord mounting the sky with wings of light.

Wilhelm reached out his arms. He felt almost as if he could touch the Sun. He felt as though he could talk to the Sun. He felt as though some One's great arms were folding around him. For once he was no longer feeling lonely. He loved being there.

After a while he knew he should go back to the house for breakfast, but for some reason he could not tell his father what had happened to him. He didn't say anything about being up early when he and his father sat down to breakfast together. He talked about other things.

Now it happened that while Wilhelm had been standing out on the hillside thinking these thoughts, his father had looked out of a window and had seen his son. The father thought to himself, "The time has come now at last. My son has really begun to wonder and to think and he is imagining some One greater than man." When the two sat down to eat breakfast, however, the father did not tell his son that he had seen him. He talked about other things.

Not long after, on a clear dark night, the father suggested that they sit out on the grass together and watch the stars. It was a beautiful evening and the sky was dotted with thousands of stars. Soon the father began telling the boy what the stars really were. He said that probably almost every one of these stars they were seeing was really a great big sun like the sun that shone each day, but since these suns were so very, very, very far away—millions and millions of miles away—they seemed like mere dots.

When Wilhelm heard these things, something hurt him inside. Such tremendous thoughts were too great for him to bear. It seemed as though his father, in telling him these things, had spoiled the greatness of his Sun, that Sun that had seemed so wonderful—his one all-powerful friend. Wilhelm felt so very badly he could not even tell his father how badly he felt.

The days went by and Wilhelm seemed to have lost his happiness. Again he was lonely in the same old way. Another clear dark night, his father once more took Wilhelm out on to the hillside in the dark and together they sat on the ground and looked up at the thousands of stars sparkling in the sky. The father asked his son to repeat all he had told him before about the stars and then he taught him even more of their greatness and wonder. Finally, the boy could stand the strain no longer and he cried out, "Father, dear Father, you have made my Sun seem small, and in his place you have put these thousands of suns. I have been believing that it was our Sun who was all-powerful, that it was he who had made us live. That he could do all the things nobody else can do. That he could help us and make us happy. Tell me, Father, who are all these other suns? Who? Why are they there? There must be some One greater than all. Some One who makes them all move together. Tell me, Father, who is he?"

Then the father told his son the very best and greatest thoughts he himself could think. He said that he, too, felt there must be some One—greater than all the suns—who in some way kept all the suns together going round and round in one great orderly, dependable way. Some One who was himself invisible, who had always been and always would be.

Then Wilhelm threw his arms around his father's neck. He could not say in words how happy he was. Together the two knelt on the grass and the father prayed. Wilhelm felt very tiny in so immeasurably large a universe of suns and planets, millions of miles around. Yet he felt at home and unafraid. As he walked back into the house with his father, Wilhelm thought to himself, "I am wiser than I have ever been before. I wonder if I ever can be any wiser."

At the end of the story the leader said, "I have told you this story because of two suggestions it has in it for us and for our work together in this Sunday School."

1. If Wilhelm were able by the time he was ten years old to figure out for himself an idea of there being God, each one of you must be old enough now to do your own thinking about God, too. Even though others have already told you what *they* think about God, it is time for you to begin to work out your own ideas. We do not expect that we shall all think alike, but we shall each respect the other's thinking so long as each one tries to be true to himself and to what he finds out.

2. During this year in our Department we shall be

learning things about this universe in which we live. We shall probably find out things we have never heard before. It may be that sometimes when you find out something new, you will feel as Wilhelm felt. Something will hurt you inside. It may seem almost as if someone were taking away from you something very important to you. If a time like that ever comes, try not to be frightened. Learning new ideas is a little like climbing a high mountain. It is hard work and sometimes it is slow going and we grow tired, but the climbers who keep on climbing until they reach the top of the mountain are the ones who get the thrill of the wonderful view. So it is as we learn more and more. The larger and more wonderful the universe becomes in our minds, the more difficult it becomes to imagine God—for one's thought of God needs to be as large a thought as all our other thoughts put together. It does hurt sometimes to try, but let us try together.

[*The outline of this story is found in* The Child's Religion, *by Pierre Bovet. London: J. M. Dent and Sons, 1928. Pages 72-78.*]

*Charles Lindbergh—The First to Risk
Flying Across the Atlantic*

One Sunday morning in the fall, before the morning session began, Connie and two other children whose names I no longer recall, found outside on the ledge of one of the windows of their classroom the body of a dead bird. They brought it to me in a mood of awe and gentleness. Connie asked if she could keep it and take it home with her. I felt the spirit of real grief in their quiet, intense manner. We stood together wondering what had happened to the bird. Had it been flying in the dark and had it bumped blindly against the church tower? Was it sick? How far had it been flying? Where had it come from? Was it on its way South with a flock of other birds?

I felt the episode was a significant one for these children, especially for Connie. I knew Connie well. She had been living with a heart heavy with resentment ever since her younger brother had been adopted into the family. She had felt lost, unloved by her parents. She still needed an extra amount of loving appreciation to make up for these months of anger. So I began pondering on how this episode might be used the next Sunday in the Departmental Meeting. If I could use it, the very fact would accent for Connie the worth of what she had done. I knew it would mean a lot to her at least; and my experience with children had led me to believe that death is a subject of importance to all children.

The telling of the Lindbergh story was the result. It was actually introduced by telling of the episode of the previous Sunday. I told them how I wished I could ask the dead bird questions, and I gave the following imaginary conversation, as if holding the dead bird's body in my hand.

Were you flying alone, beautiful bird?
Were you tired after long hours of flying?
Were you blind? Or did some hunter lame your wing?
Or did darkness hide the tall stone tower of the church?
To what heights have you soared?
In what lands had you built your nests?
In what woods did you sound your tat-a-tat-tat?

Were you ever afraid to fly, beautiful bird?
Who taught you?
What ancestor of yours first dared to drop
    from a branch and spread her wings?
For thousands of years we of our race have envied
        you the thrill of the air.  We have been
        learning your skill slowly.  How did you learn?
Did you mind dying, little bird?  Did you mind
        losing out this time?

Then I thought of another flight on a dingy May night in 1927, when a young man was flying through the black stretches of the upper air over the boisterous rolling waves of the Atlantic Ocean.  The first man to dare to fly in a plane over the Atlantic Ocean was Charles Lindbergh.  He was all alone in his small plane as he cut his way through clouds, and sleet storms and wild winds.  He was following no leader.  He was trying to do what no one had ever succeeded in doing before him.  Years had gone into his planning.  Painstakingly he had tested every tiny bit of the machinery in his engine to discover just exactly how much strain it could carry before breaking.  He had flown thousands of miles in many kinds of weather in his little plane.  He had learned by his failures and successes.  He thought he could gain the other side of the Atlantic.  But he was not sure.  He had grown convinced that the flight should be made.  He believed men should learn to fly well enough to cross the ocean.  He was willing to risk his life.  He faced the Unknown ready for either failure or success.

On that same May night in 1927 a prize fight was to take place in a great stadium in New York City.  Acres of seats were jammed with excited crowds to watch the fight.  Before the fight began a man stepped into the ring and waved his shirtsleeved arms and called for quiet. "Laaadees and Gentul-mun, I don't know what you folks believe in, or what you don't believe in, and I don't care; but slim Lindbergh is up in the air tonight some place betwen here and France. I know you're all rooting for him to win through safe. So I'm asking you to stand up, for one minute of silent prayer for him."

At once the great throng were on their feet. There was no snickering. No one rustled his feet. For a long minute 10,000 people stood with bared heads and in a dozen different languages, or in no language at all, they prayed to the Great Spirit in this universe for the safe flight of that one man.

Then when the minute had passed, the people sank back in their seats and the radio announcer spoke through the microphone to the millions of listeners staying at home. "This great audience has been standing for a minute in silent prayer for the safety of Lindbergh," he said. "I ask that you do the same."

So others in their homes quietly sent forth their wishful prayers for Lindbergh in this great adventure.

I have been thinking of these happenings that May night long ago in 1927, and I have wondered. I am going to ask you a question I have wondered about. Suppose Lindbergh had known ahead of time that he would be successful, would you think of him as being as great a man as you now think him to be? Suppose he had failed, what would you say?

I waited for their responses. Then I spoke again.

Our great moments come when we dare to do something hard needing to be done, but don't know whether we will succeed. The way we act in the presence of possible danger, since we don't know whether we will succeed, is part of our religion. We may act as cowards. We may do just what others have done and lean on their thinking. We may try to keep from taking any risks. Or we can act intelligently, finding out every single bit we can by questioning and watching and studying, and then go ahead to do the best we know, feeling that whatever happens, the Great Spirit, the Great Mind, from whom we have come, understands. Our worth will not be judged by our success, but by the way we try to do what we believe is right and good.

Some of you have thought, perhaps, that to study religion is not very interesting. Really it is the most interesting thing there is to study, because it is the story of how people have faced the things in the world they did not understand and could not be sure about. Whenever we plan ahead for tomorrow, we realize that there is something we cannot know ahead. Some have been courageous and intelligent. One big question we need to be asking ourselves over and over again is this: "What are the things worth being courageous about?"

# CHAPTER THREE

# "Living in Truth"—Both Known and Unknown

"It is the essence and beginning of religion to feel that all of our belief and speech respecting God is untrue yet infinitely truer than any non-belief or silence."

JAMES MARTINEAU [1]

Can one worship when he does not know what or whom he is worshipping? Can an adult who is himself a questioning agnostic lead in all honesty a group of children in worshipping?

## Not Merely a Modern Issue

A brief but arresting story reported by Paul in the New Testament Book of Acts illustrates the fact that modern man was not the first to feel the force of this dilemma. On his journey as a Christian missionary into Greece, Paul says he was everywhere impressed by signs of the religiousness of the Greek people. Along the roadside, and in the temples wherever he went, he found statues of gods, perhaps Zeus, Hera, Athena, Aphrodite, or Dionysus, always with altars beside them. But one day as he approached Athens, he found a shrine without a god image upon it. He read the inscription on the stone, "To God the Unknown."

Did Paul laugh at the absurdity of worshipping "an Unknown God"?—Apparently not. Instead he was touched by the religiousness expressed, for he too, as he said, had often felt the Mystery of creation, the Reality "in whom we live and move and have our being." A Mystery which, as he said, "can never be expressed in a gold or silver or stone image contrived by human hands." (Acts 17:16-34. J. B. Phillips' translation.)

As Paul pondered, however, he began to feel pity for those worshippers who did not know the nature of the God they worshipped. He thought of the great prophets of Israel. They had declared that they had personally heard God speak. They had reported God's words with certainty. So when Paul reached Athens, he used every opportunity he was given. He spoke in synagogues, and in market places, wherever anyone would stop and listen. Many became excited. Rumors of his unusual preaching reached the ears of some of the Stoic philosophers of Athens. Some joked, saying that he sounded like a "cock sparrow crowing." Others became more serious in their curiosity, and they invited Paul to come to their hall or meeting and explain his teaching directly to them all.

This brought Paul an opportunity he greatly prized. In his talk, he began by expressing his appreciation of the religiousness he observed among the Greek people. He quoted from their sacred writings. Then he told of the extraordinary experience of finding an altar without an idol, inscribed simply with the words, "To God the Unknown." He admired the man who had dared to be so original. He said that even though he felt that God was closer to him than his hands or feet, yet he also knew the feeling of reaching out for God in the hope that he might really find Him.

As a Jew, Paul had been taught to despise all idols. He could, therefore, admire the man who had built an altar without one. Yet Paul could not be satisfied with the thought that God was unknown. His missionary zeal overpowered him. He felt compelled to tell these philosophers that the God they had been ignorantly worshipping he could declare unto them. He told them that, within their own lifetime, God had revealed himself in the person of Jesus Christ, whom God had raised from the dead after he had been crucified. This proved that he was more than a mere man, that he was divine, and that in him God had been made known.

When Paul began to speak in this manner, however, some of the philosophers laughed at his reasoning. He left the hall with but one or two in sympathy with him.

The story of this remarkable episode, preserved for us for nearly 2,000 years with such simple dramatic details, suggests in bold outline three major ways in which men have been relating themselves to the all-embracing, all-enveloping Mystery ("in which we live and move and have our being") toward which the word *God* has somehow always pointed.

The first way is that of the agnostic who does not deny the reality of an all-embracing Mystery, yet who feels no value in calling it God, or in attempting to relate himself consciously to it through any means called prayer or worship. Such persons build no temples, sing no songs of adoration, address no prayers of longing to this vague unknown beyond all human imagination. To such anti-believers it seems much more sensible to spend one's time developing good relations with other human beings whom they assume can be known. The mysterious God who cannot be known, they still insist, is a figment of man's imagination, posited as living in a

supernatural realm with whom no communication is
possible.

The second way is that of the person who refuses
to admit that God is unknown or unknowable. For
these the Mystery has been removed by a special revelation, breaking through miraculously from a supernatural realm. Such persons can say that they *know*
him in whom they believe. This is the way of the
evangelist and the dogmatist. It became Paul's way
when he spoke to the Athenian philosophers. What was
unknown to them had been made known to Jesus
Christ, to the Jewish prophets, and to Paul. Such persons do not allow themselves to doubt. They feel
strong because they feel sure. Faith for them does not
mean merely living by things hoped for. It is belief
in things assuredly known.

The third way is that of the Greek worshipper who
had the originality to build an altar "To God the Unknown." It is the way of the reverent agnostic who
acknowledges that his mind or spirit is finite and
limited. Yet he is one who has seen enough and learned
enough to feel sustained in his curiosity and to lead
him to be trustful and expectant regarding what is still
beyond his grasp. He sees in the Mystery, not a wall
shutting out *all* the light, but a mist softening its rays
so that he is not totally blinded. He can enjoy the
warmth coming through the fog of doubt. Whether or
not this Mystery permeates a supernatural world, he
feels unable to say. He knows only that he has sensed
it within the natural world, and he dares to continue to
explore.

We may think of these three ways as representing
very roughly three attitudes toward the great Mystery
of our existence: the way of the anti-believer, the way

of the dogmatic believer, and the way of the reverent and inquiring believer.

Probably no person has ever represented completely or always any one of these crudely defined attitudes; yet perhaps most of us are able to identify ourselves more often with one of them than with the others. It would seem that the way of the reverent agnostic fits best the philosophy of the educator who believes in the values to be achieved through personal experiencing and questioning.

## Agnostic About What?

Our thinking, however, should not stop here. It is important that we recognize what it is that we are really agnostic about.

"I don't want to go to Sunday School any more," said Janet to her mother. "I don't believe there is a God and my teacher is all the time trying to make me, and I'm determined not to let her." It seems strange that an intelligent nine-year-old child should already have become so certain of her denial of all true meaning for the word *God*. It seems even more puzzling to learn that her well-educated mother felt no need to ask just what conception of God her daughter had in mind that she was so certain could not be true.

In our Western culture, unfortunately, too many young children have already settled on certain rather clear mental images of God without knowing why they should have accepted them as true or false, beyond the fact that they were so told. Later when they meet con-

tradictory beliefs, or when their own experiences in life
disillusion them regarding God's special care for them,
they sometimes grow resentful and even hostile in their
feelings toward God, and reject the possibility of any
belief in God, instead of rethinking their old belief in
the light of their newly found knowledge. It is not easy
to bring these prejudiced ideas out into the open since
the children probably often have some hidden feelings
of guilt about their rejections or anticipate condemna-
tion. Trying to combat such atheism, by accenting the
duty to believe, however, will usually merely augment
the force of the resistance.

Combatting mistaken beliefs as this Sunday School
teacher apparently did, by presenting another belief
with a certainty similar to that with which the older
narrower views were presented, has become increasingly
distasteful. Neither our classrooms nor our services of
worship can profitably be turned into debating societies.
Neither will a silent evasion of all the issues encourage
serious original thoughfulness. The varied ideas that
have been gathered up into this three-letter word *God*
are too pivotal in our study of religious history to be
evaded. Thoughts of God are still too dominant in our
Western society and too intimately influence our common emotional life to be disregarded.

In what spirit then and by what techniques can we
initiate and guide discussion of God among us?

## The Word *God*—A Symbol of Many Realities

First of all, the children need some help in becoming aware of the fact that all words are symbols. Some words are symbols of something definite that we can see and touch or smell. Other words are symbols of a combination of things that we put together in our minds; for example, such generalized words as *chair, boy, girl,* etc.

There are other words that symbolize not only what we can see but also our thoughts about things that we cannot see. An interesting word to talk about would be the word *America.* Do they believe in *America?* Is *America* real or make believe? What do we mean when we say *America?*

Sometimes the word symbolizes a portion of geographical territory belonging to one government. At other times the word *America* refers to the people who belong as citizens in that land, even though they may be living in some other countries. Again the word *America* may refer to both the land and the people, and even include their history, their form of government, their patterns for living, and their predominating feelings and attitudes. *America* also means certain ideal values for which soldiers are prepared to die and to which elected officers must swear to be loyal.

Is then *America* real or make believe? Is *America* just a thought? Has anyone ever seen *America?* Is

*America* a person—a he, she or it? Does *America* think, have purposes, make plans? Can anyone talk to *America?* When we sing praises to *America* are we dishonest with ourselves? Are we being superstitious? Or are we trying to express something unutterable, that seems to us to be really true? Which of these different meanings for *America* can one be agnostic about? Or which would one deny if he said "I do not believe there is any America?"

If then so simple a word as *America* has included so many meanings, what about the three-letter word *God* that has had and still has more different meanings than any other one word in the English language? A word into whose meaning has been put the meanings in all things, all life, from their beginnings to their ends, or from everlasting to everlasting, worlds without end? Meanings ranging from those that are fanciful and even absurd to those that are realistic and almost universally acceptable as true to human experience? Which of all these meanings calls for agnosticism? Which can be categorically denied? Can modern men and women simply discard *all* the meanings this word has had through the centuries, or shall they begin by looking at the multiple meanings and discriminate between them on the basis of the most accurate knowledge and the keenest understandings they can muster?

# Are We Free to Believe as We Wish?

Dr. John Baillie of England has described his own way of searching for God and the common way of many others:

Part of the reason why I could not find God was that there is that in God which I did not wish to find . . . There was a side to the divine reality that was unwelcome to me . . . It seems to me this is very commonly the case . . . We have conceived our own idea of God . . . but because there is no God corresponding to our idea, and because we are looking for none other, we fail to find the God who really is there.[2]

The kind of question for anyone to ask is not "What kind of God would I *like* to believe in? Or what kind of God was I taught to believe in? And can either of these gods be true?" The significant question to ask is, "What kind of God may actually be true in view of what I am learning about existence, about myself, and about all that is or has been or that may become possible in the future?"

No matter how much of a humanist one may be, it would seem impossible (at least to me) for a thoughtful and sincere person who is trying to be a citizen of the world, who knows sympathetically something of man's religious history, to feel it necessary to discard completely all the ideas or concepts that have at one time or another been a part of the generalized thought symbolized by the word *God*. He may call the old God dead who favored Abraham and destroyed the idol-worshipping Babylonians. He may call that God dead who sent the plagues upon the Egyptians and saved the Hebrews. He may call that God dead who died on a cross to save mankind. He may call that God dead who prospers the righteous and keeps the wicked poor, who changes the laws of Nature in order to show his power or to reward the righteous and punish the wicked. He may believe that the universe is neutral to human needs or even unjust. He may refuse to try to imagine God as belonging in a supernatural world. Nevertheless, after all such denials, there remain still other thoughts for which the word *God* has stood, and that deserve serious consideration and respect.

Or perhaps there are new meanings that now need to be embodied in the word *God*. Physicists and astronomers have never been more humble than today. What is man that he should have thought all was made for him? What are the limitations in the energies activating a never resting universe? "If we knew how to release all the energy even in one breath of air," writes William L. Lawrence, "we would have enough power to run a large airplane all the time for a year." The very thought of "the hidden likenesses" among the innumerable atoms whirling about everywhere, whether within the atoms that flow through each human body or in those flying through the distant spaces between the suns and stars, staggers all human imagination.

Furthermore, "Living organisms have purposes," says such a biologist as Edmund Sinnott. "It is as if they knew the goals for which they were striving." [3] "Evolution is a series of successive plant and animal inventions for new purposes," writes Weston La Barre, "not merely the results of chance shuffling of genes." [4]

Anthropologist Loren Eiseley writes of that "delicate, elusive *mysterious principle known as organization* which leaves all other mysteries concerned with life stale and insignificant by comparison . . . Like some dark and passing shadow within matter, it cups out the eyes' small windows or spaces the notes of a meadow lark's song in the interior of a mottled egg. That principle—I am beginning to suspect—was there before the living in the deeps of water." [5]

A modern Psalmist, "having pressed his hands against the confining walls of scientific method," sings his own reverent poetic song to the ineffable, unutterable reality, both beyond and within all. To call this by the word *God* is in no deep sense an answer. The word merely suggests that there must be an answer even though we may never know fully what it is.

To be agnostic simply to save ourselves the mental trouble of further delving or because we have grown weary of trying to think hard, or because we are afraid to run the risk of finding that life is not after all what we want it to be, may well dull our alertness in general. *The kind of agnosticism worthy of an intelligent and courageous person is the kind that is ceaselessly trying to decrease the range of its unknowing.* It is not the freedom to live in a world of his own dreaming that the person of integrity claims. It is rather a hardy freedom that insists on the liberty to dare to risk trying to live in truth.

## Akhenaten—"Living in Truth" [6]

This expression "Living in Truth" was the basic guiding principle of the theology of the unforgettable Akhenaten, the heretic Pharaoh of ancient Egypt. In many Church Schools today, boys and girls study the fascinating story of this unique religious reformer during the pre-adolescent period. To Akhenaten "Living in Truth" meant what today many would mean by "Living in God," because to Akhenaten the one Divinity deserving man's joyful worship was *Truth* itself. The new temple he built in his new capital city he did not call "The House of God" but "The Seat of Truth." For him Divinity was actual, natural, and really true. It had certain qualities of personality, yet Akhenaten never symbolized it in any anthropomorphic form of art. It was conceived of rather as a universal radiant energy that all men could feel streaming down upon them, and even into the very heart of their being.

In searching for a new symbol that would vivify this new way of conceiving God, Akhenaten decided upon the most universally experienced reality of which he could think. He rejected the stiff, giant, human figures of Amon and Re that were so evident everywhere. Nor was he satisfied with the half-animal and half-human images, such as those of Anubis and Hathor. Akhenaten returned to a very old Egyptian symbol used by the ancient philosophers, namely the Sun, on whom all life on earth is dependent; but he transformed it into a life-giving source, high above and far away, yet reach-

ing every living creature with its energizing blessing.
He transformed it into a living God who in the beginning had created all things, and who day by day is still
creating and designing millions of living forms. In writing of Aten, Akhenaten used such descriptive words as
these: "The creator of the germ in woman." "A nurse
even in the womb." "One who makes the seed into
man." The original feature in Akhenaten's symbolic
painting of Divinity is found in the many outspreading
rays that reach down from the center of radiance, like
long arms each holding in its hand the symbolic gift
of life, touching the heads and lighting the faces, as it
were, of all living beings.

To the young imaginative Akhenaten and his sensitive and artistic Queen Nefertiti, the whole universe
seemed to be filled with a kind of radiant energy, both
material and spiritual. Morning by morning the Creator was born anew and all living creatures were blessed
and made glad. They could sing and be glad and even
shout for joy and feel bound together in one great
family under these all-embracing arms. Idealistic as
the picture may seem to others, to Akhenaten and
Nefertiti it symbolized the Truth, and in this Truth
they determined to try to live.

Because they believed this to be Truth, they
changed radically many of the age-old patterns of life
by which Pharaohs had always been governed. They
built a whole new capital city, with a new and beautiful
temple whose halls for worship were unroofed so that
the beams of the rising sun could pour down upon everyone as he prayed. The royal artists decorated the walls
with realistic paintings of a wholly new kind from those
in the old temples of Thebes. The royal pair were portrayed in natural poses, with their children playing

around them. In the old paintings, the Pharaoh was
either portrayed sitting or standing alone, or if his queen
were with him she was made small, perhaps no higher
than the seat of his chair. Akhenaten and his Queen,
however, were always painted the same size, sometimes
eating together, sometimes playfully teasing each other
or kissing the babies in their arms, and always with the
over-arching symbol of Divinity touching them, their
children, and even their servants, giving to all the gift
of life.

My reason for describing Akhenaten's symbolic
expression of Divinity has not been to set it forth as
"the truth." It has been rather to emphasize the truth-
fulness of his attitude of mind. To him it seemed true;
and he risked his throne because he believed it to be
truth. With James Martineau, we can all be sure that
whatever we may say about God cannot be wholly true.
All we can hope for is that we have found at least a part
of the truth.

Since each one's outlook is partial and each one's
emotional needs are slightly different from those of
another, it is surely of great importance that we, and
the children with us, learn at least some of the different
ways in which men through the ages have imagined
Divinity. It is for this reason that we have decided to
expose children, even in their very early years, to differing points of view.

# Illustrations from Experience: Great Men Who Asked Questions

## *George Washington Carver (Four Stories)*

Since so much time is usually given in the classrooms of our schools of religion during these middle years of childhood to helping children come to know men of the ancient past, it is surely important that from time to time in the services of worship the children's interests should be directed toward ethical, social, and community problems affecting their immediate worlds. Dramatic stories appear from time to time in current papers and magazines, or some unusual event or tragedy occurs within the immediate community. In the service of worship someone may profitably review such an event, and thus initiate discussion and contemplation of the human values at stake.

At other times the leader may tell stories of significant persons not now living, but from the recent past, who perhaps pioneered, under even greater difficulties than those experienced during the children's lifetime, with the very same problems that are being stressed today.

Arousing children to join in some direct social action, or to join in giving toward the support of a needy cause can be of high value; and so also may be the building up of strong and intelligently conceived purposes. Adults and children alike develop ideals by becoming imaginatively acquainted with personalities of unusual courage and devotion. With this second type of goal in mind, I have chosen to present four stories of George Washington Carver, one of the truly great men in our nation's history, whether Negro or white be counted. The way he lived and the kinds of things he did are of the sort that appeal to boys and girls oriented in the sciences. Carver was not only a famous biochemist and an outstanding teacher, he was also a very deeply religious person. His religion grew out of a vital union of his understanding and respect for the natural world and his profound love and concern for his fellow men, especially for those who were being thwarted in their ambitions and being deprived of their common rights as human beings.

Some may be hesitant about spending four Sundays on stories of just one man, thinking that in so doing Carver is being given greater importance than he deserves. This is not the real issue. Whoever the man may be, if a biographical sketch is to be given, several stories are needed in order to bring the person to life. Enough vivid details need to be presented so that the children can identify with him in their feelings. If but one Sunday is spent on one person, it will be wiser to portray but one or two concrete episodes, such as is done with the story of Sir Isaac Newton, so that what is told is vivid enough to linger in memory and appealing enough to stir an emotional reaction.

## A Stolen Baby Exchanged for a Horse

No one knows exactly when George Washington Carver was born. We can merely say it was about one hundred years ago, while the war over slavery between the North and South was going on. George's young mother had been a slave ever since she was seventeen, when Moses Carver, a Missouri farmer, had bought her for $700. This mother and a two-year-old daughter and George, a very young baby, were living together in a one-room log cabin, set behind Moses Carver's big farmhouse.

Early one evening, the little girl and the new baby were sitting together on their mother's lap, as she rocked them in the big rocking chair and was singing them a lullaby, when suddenly the door was opened and two strange men walked right in without being invited. One dragged the mother off with the baby in her arms, put her on the back of a horse standing outside, climbed up behind her on the horse's back and drove off. The other stranger did something to the little sister so that she could not follow, and left her lying on the doorstep. Then he too drove off on another horse.

Farmer Carver, hearing screams and the pounding of horses' hooves, rushed out of his house, but he was too late. The mother and baby were gone; and the two-year-old sister lay dead on the doorstep. Quickly Mr. Carver persuaded a neighbor to chase the thieves. He untied his best horse, and told the man, "Ride as fast as you can. Bring Mary and the baby back, and I'll give you forty acres of land and the horse besides."

It was several days before the man returned. When late one evening he appeared, all he had with him was a soggy dirty bundle that he had found left under a tree in the woods. The baby inside the bundle was wheezing and coughing and seemed scarcely able to breathe. The mother was never found. Moses Carver thanked his neighbor for his trouble and gave him the horse in exchange for the baby.

The farmer's good wife took the soggy bundle into their own house and placed it in a big basket, beside the warm kitchen fire. She tore off the wet clothes, wrapped the baby in a warm dry blanket, washed his cold hands and face in clean warm water, and tried to feed him a little milk. His little body was feverish. He almost choked each time he coughed. She could see he was a very sick child.

Tenderly day and night Mrs. Carver cared for the baby. Over and over again she would say to herself, "Mary's child must live! Mary's child must live!" And he did live, but he was very slow in growing up and learning to crawl and to walk. He was still slower in learning to talk. Those weeks of coughing, it seems, had torn some of the muscles in the baby's throat so that it hurt him to make any kind of sound. As the throat slowly healed, he became able to make a few squeaky noises, but he was a boy five years of age before he was able to talk clearly enough for even Mrs. Carver to understand him.

Since George had been born a slave, because his mother was one, he was expected to begin working on the farm by the time he was six years old. Sometimes it was to help with the cooking. Sometimes it was to tend the chickens or the pigs. Sometimes it was pulling weeds in the cornfield. Sometimes it was working in Mrs. Carver's flower garden. Caring for the flowers was what George liked best.

While he was growing up on the farm, George had no playmates of his own age. The Carvers' nearest neighbors lived a mile away, and they were white farmers with white children. George was a Negro and was not allowed to play with them. So George made friends with the wild animals, the rabbits, the squirrels, and the chipmunks, and *with the flowers*. Taking a basket and a trowel, he would often wander alone into the woods and gather mosses and flowers and come back home to replant them in Mrs. Carver's garden. The animals didn't seem to mind that George couldn't talk clearly. "They talk to me," he said, "and tell me lots of things."

One morning Mrs. Carver discovered a bird's nest she had not seen before, lying on a low branch of the cherry tree. It was woven of twigs and chicken feathers and soft mosses. "What kind of a bird's nest is this?" she asked George. He smiled and said, "It's not a real bird's nest at all. I made it."

"You made it? How did you learn how?"

"The birds showed me."

"What a boy!" thought Mrs. Carver, "to dream up such an idea." It never occurred to her then that dreaming up new ideas would be what her boy would be doing all his life.

By the time he was a little over six years old, George began talking pretty well; but he would stutter if he got excited. Mr. Carver confided to his wife one day, "Sometimes I wish George couldn't talk so well. He is beginning to ask me so many impossible questions. He bothers me. What would you say, Susan, to questions like these? 'Why is grass green? What makes grasshoppers jump? Why do morning glories fold up in the afternoon? How long does it take to make a rainbow?' "

Mrs. Carver smiled. "George is smart even though he is short and his legs are spindly. He ought to be going to school before long."

Mr. Carver frowned. "There's no school around

here where a Negro boy can go. You know that, Susan. And what would he do with book learning anyway? George will always have to be a farmer."

"But, Moses, you keep forgetting. The war is over now and the South lost in the fight. We really have no longer the right to call George our slave. He doesn't seem to realize it yet, and he has nowhere else to go. He has nobody to take care of him but us. But some day, Moses, George is going to want to be free."

Moses Carver said nothing. The subject was dropped. But George's questions did not stop.

Moses Carver had a few young grapevines. It was George's special responsibility to tend them. Those little grapevine plants were special. They had come from a Swiss farmer, Herman Jaeger, who had a very large and wonderful vineyard about eight miles away.

One evening several years after, while Farmer Carver and his wife and George were sitting on the porch together, George broke their silence with one of those questions.

"Why are grapes purple?"

"I don't know," said Mr. Carver rather gruffly. "And besides all grapes are not purple. Some are green. Nobody knows why some grapes are purple and some are not."

"Does God know?" asked the weak high-pitched voice.

"Of course, God knows," said Mr. Carver solemnly.

"Then I'll ask Him," said George, and he slipped out of his chair and walked out into the garden. The farmer was startled. He was about to call George back. "Let him go," said Mrs. Carver quietly.

"But—but," protested the farmer, " 'tisn't right. He shouldn't talk that way. Why he sounded as if he were going to meet God out there, around the house!"

"Maybe he will," answered the wife. "He must learn to read the Bible for himself. He's now almost ten. You know that speller Mrs. Mueller gave him? He takes it with him to the field and he works on those words while he weeds."

"Yes, you're right. George must learn to read, and he must learn to read the Bible."

Not many weeks after this came one of George's great and unforgettable days. Moses Carver took the boy with him in his mule cart all the eight miles to Mr. Jaeger's vineyard. The first sight of the big white house and the acres and acres of grape arbors all around seemed to George like heaven itself.

Mr. Jaeger met them at the gate, and showed them around. He took them first to a long, low house with a glass roof. George had never seen such a house before. He walked down the narrow aisles between the long boxes of growing flowers. He put his head close to the flowers. He timidly touched some of the leaves. He began singing very softly or was he talking to them?

"You love plants, my boy?" said Mr. Jaeger.

"Yes, yes," said George as he stretched his arms wide. "I love everything."

The grape man took George's brown hand in his, patting it gently.

Turning to Mr. Carver, the grape man said, "The hand of a gardener, his touch will bring life."

"Come with me, my boy," he said turning to George. "I want to show you something."

So Mr. Jaeger led George to another one of the boxes. "Here are some wild grapevines. I gathered them from the side of the hill in the woods. These grapes are small and rather sour."

"But they're good," said George. "Me and the rabbits like them."

Mr. Jaeger smiled and walked on to another box. "Here are some grapes from Virginia. The grapes on these are very sweet and large, but the stems are weak and thin, and the vines rot easily, and the grapes are not juicy. Now watch me. I'm going to help these two kinds of grapevines to grow together so that they can help each other."

Mr. Jaeger then cut a twig, with a tender bud on its tip end from one of the Virginia grapevines; and from one of the wild grapevines he also cut a twig about the same size. The part he cut off from this wild vine he threw away. Then Mr. Jaeger took out his pocket knife and carefully cut the lower end of the twig from the Virginia vine until he had pointed it nearly like a pen. He laid this twig carefully down on the earth for a moment. Then he went back to the wild grapevine, and holding the cut end of the twig, he began cutting it out carefully, making a kind of open cup into which the pointed end of the other twig from the Virginia vine would fit. Then he fitted the Virginia twig on the wild vine. As he held them together tightly, he bound them together with a small rag and some string, just as a surgeon might bind together two parts of a broken bone.

"Now," said the grape man, "these two plants, I think, will grow together into one plant. The wild-vine part will make the stems strong, and the Virginia-grape part will make the grapes sweet and large and juicy. We call this *grafting* two kinds of plants together. So God and I work together making better grapes."

Mr. Jaeger then led George to the door of the greenhouse, and showed him acres of grapevines. "We will ship grapes from these vines to all parts of the country and even to other lands. You see these hills all around. They all belong to God. All the earth is God's." Then looking down into the boy's eyes, he added: "And this God, this great and good God, my boy, is your Father."

"My—my—Father!" stammered George.

"Yes, you are one of his children, like all the small animals in the woods. Even though they tell you that you have no father and mother, you have God." Then taking the small boy's hand in his once more, he said: "God has given you a grower's hand, George. You too must work as I do with God."

George felt the sunshine reaching down into his heart. Before he and Mr. Carver said good-bye, Mr. Jaeger brought him a Bible and put it in his hand. George opened the book and tried to read it, but he could not read more than a few words. Tears began to come to his eyes.

"Take it. It is yours, my boy. Already you know much that others do not, for you *see* more. Many people only *look*. They do not *see*. You *see*, my boy. Some day you will be able to read this book. You must read all books. And the Creator will teach you many things."

George Washington Carver was ten years old on that unforgettable day, but he felt much older and bigger. He had decided. He would go wherever he needed to go in order to learn to read. He would read many books. He would work with the Creator, as the grape man did.

*All for the Sake of an Education*

We shall begin our story of George Washington Carver again just one week after that unforgettable day he spent with the grape farmer where he had seen those acres and acres of wonderful grape vines. All week long George had been living with his memories of that great experience.

"All the earth is God's. This great and good God is your Father. You are one of his children, just like all the animals in the woods. You must work as I do with the Creator. . . . Some day you will be able to read this book. You will read all books." Over and over again George seemed to hear the grape man speaking to him.

George had made up his mind. He would go to school no matter what had to be done in order to do so. He would work with the Creator. He must learn how.

"But the nearest school is eight miles away," said Farmer Carver. "If you stay here with us and work on our farm we will give you a home as long as we live, and we will take care of you. If you leave us, you will have to take care of yourself. We can give you no help."

George Washington Carver was determined. He would be free and he would get an education. So just one week after that visit to Jaeger's vineyard, this ten-year-old Negro boy said good-bye to the only two friends he had. With a few belongings tied in a shawl on a rod and slung over his shoulder, he started off barefooted and alone, to walk the eight miles to the nearest town and school where a Negro child could go.

During the weeks that followed he slept on the hay in a barn loft. He rose early each morning to go to school, and after school was over he went from door to door asking for work to do so that he would not starve.

After months sleeping on the hay, he was given a room in a shed which someone helped him to furnish with a bed and chair and table. So the boy advanced year by year from one grade to the next until he had learned all that this elementary school could teach him. But this was not enough. So off he ventured again to find a high school to which he could go and learn. But no high school in the state of Missouri would admit a Negro student. This time the young man would have to walk at least sixty miles into the state of Kansas where he had been told that Negroes were admitted to the public high schools.

Again George was with strangers. He had the same hard kind of day-by-day struggle all over again: living in some small back room, taking in washing, weeding gardens, cooking, washing pots and pans, and scrubbing floors. In fact, he did any kind of work anyone would let him do, so that he could keep on going to school.

But George found here and there a few wonderful friends. Some were Negroes and others were white people. There were Aunt Maria and Uncle Andy, for example, in whose small cabin he lived for a whole year helping Maria with her laundry and cooking. There was also Mrs. Martins who had taught him to play the piano, while he had taught her how to tend her flower garden. There were the Mulhollands who discovered the young man's paintings, and wanted him to study art and become an artist.

Never well dressed, George Carver seemed to most people just another *"darky."* It was the rare person now and then who caught the bright gleam in his dark eyes and encouraged him to go on to school. It was they who made the long days and years bright with hope.

Finally this ambitious young man graduated from high school, but still this was not enough. He was determined to go on to college. He would work with the Creator, but he must learn better how to do it. So he wrote a letter to the president of the nearest college, Highland University, asking to be admitted, and received in response a letter of acceptance.

Then came another good-bye to all his friends, and a third long walk, this time to find the college. At the end of this journey came the most bitter disappointment of all. He called on the president of Highland University expecting to be admitted.

"But you didn't say in your letter that you were a Negro," said the President. "We've never had a Negro student in our college. I simply can't take you."

The big white man in his chair must have seen the disappointment on George Carver's face. "But why do you want to college?" he asked. "You've finished high school. For a Negro that's very good indeed. What would you do with a college education anyway? It seems to me it would be wasting your time and ours for you to spend four years in college. What work could you do at the end that would be any better than what you can do now?"

George Carver's answer was brief, "Time belongs to God, sir. I am going to college because there is work for me to do. I must be ready."

Then the search for more education began all over again. George Carver was still determined he would find a college somewhere that would admit him as a student. He finally discovered one, but it was again miles away in the State of Iowa. Young Carver spent several more years waiting and working on a farm before he was able to begin his schooling again.

At last came the great and happy day of his graduation from the State University at Ames, Iowa! How the big audience clapped when he was given his diploma, the only Negro in all the university!

Before the day was over there came word from the university president that he, once a motherless Negro slave, was to become one of the teachers in this very university. He was to be one of the university faculty! He was to teach botany and have charge of the greenhouses! How wonderful for him were those next two years!

Then came the letter from Booker T. Washington, President of Tuskegee Institute, a new small school for Negroes in far away Alabama. The writer of the letter had never seen Mr. Carver. He had only heard him spoken of as a very promising educated young Negro who could teach men to farm with their minds as well as their plows. "He can make corn grow on a boardwalk," said a joking friend.

Young Carver had, however, often heard of Booker T. Washington, the great Negro educator, once himself a slave and now president of this new school that he, himself, had started especially for Negroes in the South.

In his letter, Mr. Booker Washington wrote:

The children come barefoot. They walk for miles over bad roads. They are thin and in rags. You could not understand such poverty, Professor Carver. These people do not know how to plow, to plant or to harvest. I am not skilled at such things. I teach them to read, to write, to make good shoes, good bricks, and to build walls. I cannot teach them to grow food and so they starve.

I cannot offer you money, position, or fame. I am asking you to give all these up. I offer you in their place hard work, hard, hard work, the task of bringing a people from degradation, poverty, and waste to full manhood."

Young Carver read the letter over and over again. Another decision had to be made. At the university in Ames his dreams were now coming true. He was teaching both white and Negro students how to work with the Creator. He had a well-equipped greenhouse. He had already been offered a fine position as a professor in another state university, which he had refused. What ought he to do?

Then came the afternoon when he tore a small piece of paper from a tablet on his desk and wrote three words, "I will come," and signed his name. He put the paper in an addressed envelope, and mailed it to Dr. Washington.

## A Pioneer Professor of Biochemistry

Mr. Carver never regretted his decision to go to Tuskegee. He didn't mind being poor. He would have enough to eat. He had a place to sleep in quiet, and he would have a chance to work with his Creator.

What young Carver *did mind,* however, was that he was given no laboratory in which to work; only a big bare room with a few tables and chairs. What he *did mind* was not having any land in which to plant seeds except a small, bare, grassless campus and no greenhouse at all.

The first day he met his class he said to the students, "We must have a laboratory where we can do experiments. We're going to do something about it right away today, even though it is something that has never been done before. We will go from house to house in the town of Tuskegee, and we will beg for scraps, things thrown away as junk, that we can use in our laboratory. You'll ask for kitchen pots and pans, tea kettles and sieves, pails, bottles and jars, lamps and gas burners, wood, boxes, tubes, and pipes."

When all these things had been collected Mr. Carver added his own fine personal microscope which had been the loving parting gift from the students and faculty in Iowa. So together, he and his students furnished what he called "God's little workshop." He set the students right to work gathering mosses and weeds and even clay and soil from the woods nearby. They began mashing them, boiling them, separating them into parts, to discover what they were made of and to think of ways to use them.

Professor Carver himself, it is said, used to rise very early every morning and walk out into the woods alone before breakfast. He would bring back perhaps a basket of wild flowers or a pail of clay. One day soon after his arrival he stumbled and fell into a swamp. He tried to wash the dirt off from his trousers and hands, but to his surprise he found a blue stain on his hand that would not come off. He was delighted. "I've learned a secret," he whispered to himself. "There are paints in this clay." He began to see other colors in other clay: red, yellow, brown.

When he got back to his laboratory he sifted out the small stones. He mashed what was left in burlap bags, he mixed it with warm water and shook it till all the water was discolored. Then he separated the water from the clay. He mixed a little oil with the clay and, lo and behold, he had paint!

Carver and his students made many colors of paint from the clay in the hills. They collected it in jars. They painted tables and walls. One day they even painted the whole outside of a little church in the village.

When alone in the evening he would often paint pictures of the mountains he remembered from his childhood, and of many flowers of the woods. Every day, all the rest of his life, he wore a flower in his buttonhole. He would wear the same old suit and cap he had worn for years, but the flower in his buttonhole was always fresh every day.

All the new things he thought of doing were very interesting to the students; yet his most important work had scarcely begun. The farmers of Alabama were indeed very poor, the white families as well as the Negroes; and they had been getting poorer year by year because a little worm, called the boll-weavil, had come from somewhere and had begun eating the white cotton blossoms as soon as they came out. The cotton became brown and rotted before it ripened. It became useless and could not be sold. What could the cotton farmers do? Everybody had been raising cotton and nothing but cotton for years.

"Why not try raising some other kind of crop that the boll-weavils will not eat up? Why not rotate your crops?" asked Carver. "Why not try raising peanuts for example, for a while?" At first this seemed silly. "Raise peanuts! Who wants peanuts except at the circus?"

But the farmers were desperate and a few began

planting peanuts. Mr. Carver's students were given a twenty-acre field on the campus where they could experiment. After a year had passed they made exhibits of the peanuts that could be grown on an acre of land. It was really exciting for a while, but after several years there got to be too many peanuts! The farmers couldn't get enough money for them to make it pay to raise them. Again they were growing poorer and poorer. What could they do?

Carver was really discouraged this time. He was afraid he had made a big mistake. He went to his laboratory and refused to talk to any one. He must be left alone with God. The whole earth belonged to God. Surely there was some new way.

The next morning he asked his students to bring him a bushel basket full of peanuts to the laboratory. When they had brought enough, he thanked them, and shut the door. That evening they saw his light burning throughout the whole night. They took his breakfast to him in the morning, but he would not let them into the room. When someone tapped on the door, he called, "Go away! We're busy."

"Why does he say *We?* None of the students is with him. None of the teachers is there. He is all alone. Why does he say *We?*" This lasted six days and through the nights as well. Finally late on the evening of the sixth day, he climbed the stairs to his room and flung himself across his bed and slept.

The next morning he called his students back to the laboratory. What did they see? Bottles and bottles on the tables and shelves all filled. "Here is milk made from peanuts," he said. "Here is oil. Here is a powder; here a cold cream to rub on the face. Here is a peanut coffee." He showed them about twenty different kinds of useful things he had made from the peanuts. He let the students taste the milk and he asked them to experiment with making bread out of the flour.

"How in the world did you do it, Dr. Carver?" someone asked. So he told them his story.

"I was desperate. I felt I needed to know something no one had ever yet found out. I began talking to myself and to God. I asked God, 'Dear Mr. Creator, please tell me what the *universe* was made of.' "

"The Great Creator answered me: 'Little man, ask something more in keeping with that little mind of yours. Ask something more nearly your size.' "

"So then I asked, 'Please, Mr. Creator, I want to know all about the *peanut*.' 'That's better!' I felt Mr. Creator saying, 'You can never know all about peanuts, but you can learn a great deal if you will take even a handful of peanuts and study them. You are a chemist. Take the peanut apart and find out for yourself what it has been made of.' "

"So that was why I asked you, my students, to bring a bushel of peanuts to our laboratory. I felt I had to work alone, with only God beside me, so as to make sure of what I was discovering. When I became sure, I called you to come and see."

So it had come about that the small slave boy, who once thought he could talk with the wild squirrels and rabbits and birds and flowers, when he became a man learned how to listen with the mind of a scientist to what peanuts could tell him. He discovered that the little peanut plant was really a biochemist too like himself, without knowing it; for the peanut plant somehow could take apart the air and the earth. It could separate the oxygen, hydrogen, carbon in the air, and the minerals in the ground, and mix them up together again so that they were changed into more complicated things; into sugar and starch and oil and proteins, which the peanut plant could eat and turn into peanuts!

Later on Professor Carver and his students with him learned how to make over three hundred different kinds of things out of peanuts! When a museum was provided on the campus, he and his students arranged exhibits of the things they had made. There were bottles and jars of peanut coffee, bleaches, a tan remover and dyes, artificial rubber, metal polish, a rubbing cream especially good for infantile paralysis victims, a peanut milk that during World War I saved hundreds of starving African babies in the Congo, even buttermilk and cheese, and the first substitute for butter— later called "oleomargarine." Professor Carver also discovered how to make paper and linoleum and wallboard from the shells and the stems. These are but a few of the three hundred items in the long list.

Professor Carver was often called "The Wizard of Tuskegee," but he disliked the name. He said he was merely finding out a few of "God's secrets" that had been hidden away in peanuts, and in the earth and air and growing things everywhere. "I do not do these things myself. The Creator does them. I am not a wonder worker. The wonders are all around us if only we would teach our eyes how to see them."

What Professor Carver did with peanuts made him famous, but this was only a small part of his discoveries. So there is still more to the story.

*"The Worst Start and the Best Finish"*

"If I were asked what living man had the worst start and the best finish, I would say 'Dr. Carver.' " A magazine writer in England wrote these words after he had seen Professor Carver honored in London as a Fellow of the Royal Society of England and given a doctor's degree by the college he first attended.

Some of the folks back home in Tuskegee, however, had a rather different opinion about the Tuskegee professor. When they met him carrying his pail or his botany tin on his way to the woods, they thought he looked like a beggar. During all the forty years he had been teaching at Tuskegee, Professor Carver continued to live alone in the same two or three small rooms in the dormitory. He insisted on scrubbing his own floors because he had invented the soap and wanted to see for himself how well it worked.

Some of the students, however, would follow him about as if he were a magnet. They thought, "Perhaps he will pick up a stone or find a flower while we are with him, and he will tell us what he knows about them." Sometimes he would ask them to stand still for ten minutes and look only at the small piece of ground that was not more than five feet away from them. Then he would tell them to go back to their rooms and write down what they had seen.

In his laboratory, he studied a great many other things besides peanuts. What he and his students found out about sweet potatoes was perhaps as important as what they learned about peanuts. The sweet potato flour he taught bakers to make made it possible for thousands of people to have bread to eat during the First World War. He also showed farmers how to make a good kind of starch from the small and unsalable little potatoes. He discovered how to make a kind of breakfast food and a delicious sweet potato syrup.

During the war he was invited to come to Washington to show the army bakers and mess hall directors how to make sweet potato flour and sweet potato syrup and how to dry sweet potatoes so that they would keep. At first some of the army men doubted what a Negro could do for them, but when Professor Carver actually baked some loaves of bread using sweet potato flour in them, and they tasted it, they were convinced. Before the war was over, many army camps were mixing sweet potato flour and wheat flour, half and half, to make bread for the soldiers; and Southern farmers began making plans to plant more acres of sweet potatoes than ever before.

Professor Carver said again and again: "If all other foods were destroyed, a person could live on sweet potatoes and peanuts alone; for between them they are able to supply man with all the vitamins and all the kinds of food needed for keeping healthy."

Professor George Carver, however, did not confine his teaching to the Tuskegee Institute students and to the army bakers in Washington. He was given what was called a "Movable School." At first this was a wagon drawn by a single horse. Later it was a large automobile. Professor Carver would use it during vacation time. He would carry all sorts of samples in this automobile to show the Negro farmers in the country. He would hold meetings in their homes or in the village halls. He showed them how they could make laundry starch and flour and syrup out of sweet potatoes, and how they could dry the potatoes so they would not rot when stored away in the winter.

He would sleep in their small homes, eat with them, and joke with them, and as he was leaving he might give them some seeds to start a flower garden. He showed them how important it was not to waste anything. Out of sawdust and a vegetable dye and a little glue, he had learned to make rock as hard and beautiful as marble. Out of cotton stalks, that were usually left to rot in the fields, paper could be made and even fibers which, when dyed, could be woven into beautiful rugs. He showed them how most farmers waste enough fat each year to make all the soap their families could use. Dr. Carver was very emphatic about not wasting things.

He told the peanut farmers not to throw away the peanut shells or to burn them. He had found they could be pulverized, and sold in sacks for fertilizer that was better than the peat moss most of them used.

The farmers in the South began not only raising peanuts and sweet potatoes, but factories were being built all over the South where these different products that Dr. Carver exhibited could be made and sold. Slowly, poor Negro farmers learned to grow many things beside cotton and many poor white farmers became rich men.

A well-to-do grower of peanuts in Florida at one time found that his peanut plants were withering before they had peanuts. He couldn't figure out what was wrong. He sent samples of the plants to Tuskegee's "plant doctor," as Carver was called, who for all these many years had been studying the kinds of *bacteria* that made plants sick. Professor Carver examined the samples sent to him from the Florida farmer. He discovered the bacteria that had been the troublemakers.

He sent the man a letter telling him what needed to be done. The farmer was so grateful, he sent Dr. Carver a check for $100.00 and said he would send the same amount every month if he would be willing to keep on giving him advice from time to time. But Dr. Carver sent the check back, saying: "God doesn't charge anything for growing peanuts. I could not charge for curing them."

Thomas Edison found out about Dr. Carver's remarkable work. He sent a man down to Tuskegee to try to persuade the Professor to come up to New Jersey and help him in his electric laboratory. "Tell Carver for me," he said, "together we can unlock the universe. His limited facilities hamper him. Here we have everything with which to work." Edison offered Dr. Carver a salary greater than the salary the President of the United States was getting, but Dr. Carver said, "My work is here, in Tuskegee. I decided to give my services to help the South and especially to help my people here. This I shall do till the end comes."

Just eight years before Dr. Carver died, the younger chemists all over the country who had been studying the chemistry of plants (as Dr. Carver had been doing for thirty and more years before they began) organized a society in Dearborn, Michigan, where Henry Ford lived. It was at their annual meeting two years later that Henry Ford first became acquainted with Dr. Carver, and from that time on after Edison's death, Dr. Carver took the place of Edison in Mr. Ford's mind as "the greatest living scientist."

After that, Henry Ford used to visit often with Dr. Carver in his little rooms at Tuskegee, or invite him to come to his Florida summer home where he built a special cottage for his Negro friend. They used to sit and talk together by the hour. Ford had been once a poor boy himself and he too had done some things that nobody before him had ever thought of doing. He could understand Dr. Carver's yearning to work with the Creator, but he couldn't persuade the professor to leave Tuskegee.

During the forty years of Dr. Carver's teaching at Tuskegee, the college grew from a small school, with a few small buildings built mostly by the students themselves, until it became a large college with many fine buildings and a campus with more than a thousand students. Dr. Carver had a good laboratory in which to work, a greenhouse, and acres of land on which to experiment.

Henry Ford also had a hospital built on the campus especially for Negro children who had been crippled by infantile paralysis. He named the hospital in honor of Dr. Carver. There today they still use Dr. Carver's famous peanut cold cream for massaging paralyzed arms and legs. It is still one of the few hospitals in the South where Negro children so crippled can be cared for.

The scientists have learned many things since George Washington Carver's time. There are hundreds of factories where many kinds of plants, leaves, fruits, wood from trees, and even dirt, are taken apart, melted with very hot fires, the juices squeezed out, and what is left changed into entirely different things. Dr. Carver and Henry Ford used to talk together and dream together of the time when automobiles would be made out of plants mixed with a few treasures from the soil, such as iron, tin, and aluminum. This dream has already come true, and even more. The many colored plastics used in making toys, dresses, tables, and hundreds of things we enjoy have all been discovered since Dr. Carver began as a pioneer to make things out of weeds and peanuts and sweet potatoes and cotton.

But many of these discoveries have been made by men in the hope of making money and of getting rich. Dr. Carver's discoveries were made so that those who were starving, sick, or living in ugliness might enjoy and use the good things in God's world.

He might have patented a number of his ideas and made a lot of money. He might have become one of the world's richest men; but he chose to stay poor, to live simply, to dress simply, and to work simply with the Creator. His riches he found everywhere in the earth, in all growing things. He became rich in the love and gratitude of thousands of people whom he encouraged to find out for themselves what things are made of, and to make better use of them.

The facts contained in these stories have been gathered primarily from the following books:

*George Washington Carver: An American Biography* by Rackham Bolt, Garden City, N.Y.: Doubleday & Company, Inc., 1943.

*Dr. George Washington Carver: Scientist* by Shirley Graham and G. D. Lipscomb, Julian Messner, 1944.

*Carver's George: A Biography of George Washington Carver* by Florence C. Means, Boston: Houghton, Mifflin, 1952.

The filmstrip, *The Carver Story* can be obtained from Artison Productions, Hollywood, California. We advise, however, if any such material is shown that it be used at a final session, after the stories have been told and lived with.

## Sir Isaac Newton—Who Asked Questions of Common Things

Did you ever have the experience of playing on an ocean beach, and then for a moment stopping your play? Perhaps you stood up and looked for a few quiet moments out over the far reaches of water spread out before you seemingly without end. Did you feel very small in a very, very big world? I'm just wondering if you ever had an experience something like that because I am going to tell the story of a very great man who had just that kind of experience. Some of you have probably already heard his name, for he has sometimes been called "the greatest genius that ever lived."

Isaac Newton was born a little over three hundred years ago on a farm in the small village of Woolsthorpe, England. The boy never saw his father because Mr. Newton died before his son was born. As a boy Isaac lived on the farm with his mother alone. When he was old enough to go to the village school his teacher thought that this Newton boy was not very bright. He really did rather poor work in school. When he finally finished all the grades in this village school his mother decided he was not a bright enough boy to go on to the university to study. So she kept him at home working on the farm. She assumed that he would become a farmer such as his father had been.

Fortunately, however, she was finally persuaded to change her mind. She discovered that the trouble with Isaac was not that he was dull, but that he didn't find the books he studied in the village school as interesting as were all the natural things in the outdoors around.

Although he didn't ask his school teachers questions, he was always asking questions of the drugstore keeper. Although he wasn't fond of pulling weeds from the garden, he was always curious about the wild animals in the woods. And he was always experimenting with some new invention.

For instance, he made a toy windmill which didn't need to wait for the wind to blow to start the wheel whirling around. He did this by catching a mouse and putting it in a closed box where there was a treadwheel. The mouse seemed to enjoy running over the wheel, and the wheel was kept going around most of the time. Isaac also made kites of many different shapes and sizes and experimented with them.

Isaac Newton also began experimenting to find a way to measure how fast the wind blew. One afternoon instead of working on his spelling lesson he worked out this experiment. He went out to an open field behind the house. He marked a spot on the ground and stood on it, facing in the direction the wind was blowing. Then he jumped as far as he could and marked the spot where he landed. He turned around and faced against the wind. Again he jumped as far as he could and marked the spot where he landed. Then he measured the lengths of the two jumps. He subtracted the shorter jump from the longer one. His jump against the wind he found was shorter than his jump with the wind. He called this a measure of the strength of the wind. He did this experiment over and over again, day after day, until he could say, "This morning there is a one-foot wind." Or again he might say, "This morning the wind is only a six-inch wind."

Isaac did so many interesting things as a boy and cared so little about farming that his mother finally

decided to send him to the Cambridge University to
study. It was not long before the professors recognized
that he was really a bright young man. In fact, before
he graduated they said that Newton was better at figur-
ing with numbers than anyone else in the university.

But Isaac Newton's study at the university was
interrupted because an epidemic of a very serious kind
broke out in the college. It was called the black plague,
and thousands of people died from it. Because 300
years ago no doctors knew how such sicknesses were
caused, and no serum injections had been thought of, it
was decided to close the university until the epidemic
died down. So for two long years Isaac Newton had to
stay on the farm and work.

A famous story is told of a day when he saw an
apple fall from a tree in the orchard. Perhaps he was
gathering apples to put away for the winter. When he
saw this apple tumble from one of the branches, Isaac
Newton's curiosity began working. He remembered the
story of how Galileo had experimented by dropping
balls from the Leaning Tower of Pisa. He remembered
how Galileo had carefully worked out just how fast the
balls fell to the ground. Whether they were heavy or
light made no difference. Galileo had worked this out
so carefully that he could say it in numbers. The first
second a ball falls just so much, the second it falls so
much more, and the third second it falls still faster, and
so on. Galileo had said this speeding of the fall was
because the earth pulled things down toward it, and
the strength of the pull he called "gravity."

As Isaac Newton noticed the apple fall that afternoon, he began to ask himself other questions. He
looked up at the sky, and there he saw the moon shining
above him. He wondered, "Why is it that the moon

does not tumble down as this apple did? What is it that keeps it going round and round the earth?"

Now if Isaac Newton had asked the neighbors in the village that question they probably would have said to him, "God put the moon up in the sky. God told the moon to go round and round the earth, and the moon is obeying God. Or perhaps an angel is pulling the moon around."

Isaac Newton, however, was not satisfied with these answers. He thought that some greater plan must be in the mind of God. As he wondered and thought he made a great big guess. Perhaps this pull of the earth that Galileo called "gravity" reaches all the way to the moon, but the moon is so many miles away that the pull of the earth's gravity is not strong enough to make the moon tumble down out of the sky. It is only strong enough to pull it down enough to make it go round in a circle.

Now scientists in Isaac Newton's time had already figured out, as they thought, how big the earth was. They had decided it was about 21,000 miles in circumference at the equator. They also had measured, as they thought, how far away the moon was from the earth, about 250,000 miles away. So Isaac Newton went into the house and up to his own room and started to work out a very long and hard example in arithmetic. He began to figure out how far the moon would fall toward the earth each day for a whole month. When he finished working out this example, he found that his answer said that the moon would go around the earth in thirty-two days.

But this answer was wrong. The moon takes only twenty-eight days to go around the earth, and Isaac Newton was very much disappointed. He realized that something was wrong, but he did not know just where the mistake was. So he put his papers away in a drawer, and he began to be curious about other things.

The years went by. He went back to the university to study, and he became a professor himself. In fact sixteen years passed before Isaac Newton worked again on that arithmetic problem about the moon. Then one day a visitor from France reported to him that a scientist in Paris had found out that the old measurement of the earth was wrong. Instead of being 21,000 miles around at the equator, it was 25,000 miles around.

When Isaac Newton heard this news, he became very much excited. He rushed to his room, forgot to eat dinner, and began to work again on the long arithmetic problem he had done sixteen years before. But, it is said, he became so excited he couldn't figure straight. He kept making mistakes! This man who was famous for being the greatest mathematician in the university couldn't add or divide without making mistakes! Finally he went to a friend and said, "I'm too nervous. Please finish the problem for me." The friend did so, and after some days the answer came that Newton was looking for. According to the law of gravity, the moon ought to take 28 days to go around the earth! And it does just that!

This was one of the great moments in history. Isaac Newton and his friend lived, as it were, in a dreamland of excitement. Finding the answer to this one question seemed to open the door to many, many more questions: "Why does the earth move around the sun? Why do the other planets go on their rounds? Does everything have "gravity?" Do all the planets and stars pull one another together just so far and no farther? Is there one rule or law by which all the stars and all the planets move? Do all things everywhere happen according to some planned orderliness?"

If so, how different the world and everything everywhere was from what people had so long supposed! No longer could it be true that an angel kept the moon from falling and pulled it around the earth as men had so often said. It was *gravity*, and *gravity* could be measured! Is *gravity* in the sun too? And does the sun's *gravity* keep our earth whirling around it? Why don't the stars fall down on us? Is there *gravity* in everything, large and small, pulling things together, but not so close together that they smash into one another? Isaac Newton had changed man's picture of the universe more than Galileo had changed it when he showed that the earth was circling around the sun. Isaac Newton's picture of the universe was startling. It was puzzling, too. Where was God, then, and weren't there angels any more? Each question, answered correctly, seemed to lead on to another question, and gave a new clue for answering it.

Isaac Newton was slow in writing down what he had discovered. The book he finally wrote describing his findings is called *Principia*. It has been regarded by some as being one of the ten greatest books ever written, since it gave mankind, as it were, a new key by which to open new doors to more understanding of the universe.

Before Isaac Newton died he was highly honored. Now after over three hundred years, stories of his discoveries are still retold throughout the world. We call him one of mankind's greatest scientists and one of the world's great men. But Newton thought of himself very humbly. He felt that what he had learned was only a very small beginning of what there was still to learn.

When he was an old man, and his friends were talking about him one day, he said this: "I know not what people may think about what I have discovered. For myself, I feel that I have been like a child playing on the seashore, now finding some prettier pebble or more beautiful shell than my companions, while the unbounded ocean of truth lies undiscovered before me."

# CHAPTER FOUR

# Man's Age-old and Enduring Questions

"Religion does not fail us in the unanswered question,
For it is that question;
And it does not fail us in the time of tragedy,
For it is the spirit by which we recognize tragedy and repudiate
its finality.

.     .     .

It is the insistence within the heart that man must not be
alone in his dark.
It is the hunger, as well as the cry that hunger be fed."

ROBERT T. WESTON [1]

In the great religions, especially those of the Western world, the accent has been upon beliefs and convictions, rather than upon questioning. In fact the distinguishing marks between the different religious sects have been, for the most part, the differences in their beliefs. Although beliefs are important we need to remind ourselves that they are the fruits of experience, and that in the natural world each new life begins with its own seed. As parents of children and as educators, we need to practice looking beneath the convictions to find the earlier experiences that awakened the questions which in turn called forth the answers given as convictions.

Archibald MacLeish expressed the situation in two pertinent lines in one of his plays.

"We have learned the answers, all the answers;
It is the questions we do not know." [2]

As a result of the common urge to give directly to growing children the moral and religious convictions inherited from revered ancestors and parents, many of us have erred unwittingly by telling the answers too quickly before the children have had experiences of their own leading them to ask the kinds of questions that in the past led to these answers. The children, therefore, are often left thinking that the beliefs are not of much relevance to them. This misfortune is compounded when the answers have been given as coming from some unquestioned authority, so that the children see no need to raise questions or to examine their own experience. Later during adolescence when they have enough baffling experiences to stir their questions, the emotional trauma involved in the possible need to revise their beliefs may be beyond endurance.

## Both Conservers and Reformers

This emphasis upon strong convictions in religious matters is understandable. Those questions which we usually designate as religious, namely, questions that reach out toward what we call "Universals" and "Ultimates," are the ones that have mattered the most. The hazards of existence and the continual blending of the unexpected in experience with the dependable, of pain with ecstasy, of death with life, have made men feel keenly the need for protection and understanding and for some over-balancing good to be sure about. The mysterious powers men early sensed as hidden and active beneath the surface of things intrigued their curiosity, but at the same time they were frightening. It is still so. Living is dangerous. When any of us once becomes assured of some comforting belief, we are loath to abandon the support and assurance it brings. As Emerson wrote, however, "Men wish to be settled; only so far as they are unsettled is there help for them." [3]

Such a readiness to be unsettled, however, is difficult to accept. It requires a depth of "faith" in the cosmos that is beyond the limitations of worded assurances. It is because some great scientists have had this deep faith in the basic nature of the cosmos that they have had the courage to question old postulates. They have been willing to ponder their doubts, remain uncertain, examine more data, and search more painstakingly, even to invent instruments that would augment their powers to see and hear and so increase their range for discovering.

As a result, not a few of the world's scientists are among the most reverently religious of us. Not a few of them are among the most effective, ethical prophets, basing their teachings not primarily upon the commandments given by men of old, but rather upon their own most recent acquired insights into the very nature of existence, experienced in the here and the now on the planet earth, and in its skies.

# How Then Encourage Questioning in Religion?

A questioning and adventuring mind seems to be quite natural among younger children who are given a reasonable degree of security and affectionate care. Unfortunately, however, it has been found that through the processes of education their native tendency to be curious is sometimes dulled. How can we encourage children to keep their minds alert and questioning as long as life lasts? This would seem to be a crucial issue for those concerned with children's religious development.

The problem, however, is first of all an adult one. It is we who are most in need of change. At least I found it so in my own experience. In trying to recall my own childhood in a devout and studious Christian home, I realize that I was not wholly an unquestioning child religiously; yet, having been so surrounded by the customs and beliefs of Christianity, the questions I thought of to ask were directed not primarily toward real situations, people and things, but toward the beliefs that I was absorbing from the religious instruction given me in both church and home. My own actual experiences were so overlayed with these assumed beliefs that I could not see them in their own nakedness. When as a woman I was more deeply challenged to look directly at "real life situations" without their doctrinal coverings, I found I had to learn to ask new kinds of questions.

It meant becoming more interested in people and things directly around me, asking imaginative questions of them, wondering about stories hidden within facts. It meant learning to ask questions of common things right before my eyes, anywhere. My religion had been so idealistically pointed toward a better future that I had almost lost respect for the present. Furthermore, it had been so tightly wrapped up in principles to be followed that the concrete realities before me and within me were veiled. In order to companion growing children in real life situations day by day, I had to learn to live more vividly myself in the here and now.

Furthermore, my ethics had been linked so predominantly with interhuman values that I found myself overlooking the ethics involved in my relationship with other living creatures and with *things*. God had been so much "out of this world" above and beyond and behind it, that I had not developed a lively sense of the immediacy of "the infinite" and "the eternal" within this present cosmos. For this reason when my interest in helping children awakened, I found I needed to develop new habits, one of which was the habit of asking questions of common things and discovering their unspoken stories. One of Carl Sandburg's choice poems aroused me. It begins with the words, "If one egg could speak." The story which he thinks he could hear touches infinity.

Geologists have grown skilled in reading such stories in stones and rocks and in mountains of sand and clay. Archaeologists have learned to read the language of carbon isotopes deposited in ancient bones and in the relics of primitive human artifacts. Biologists with the help of those amazing electron microscopes, and as a result of their patient observations of developing embryos, have been able to report new findings regarding the mysteries of birth and inheritance.

The amazing advances made in psychological and physical therapy are due to the questioning eyes and minds of persevering men and women who refused to be content with the old assumptions.

Although all of us can not be professional scientists,

yet we may all cultivate more consciously the habit of seeing with questioning minds and with questioning eyes.

In order to encourage in ourselves the pursuit of questioning minds in religion, let us for a while contemplate the history of mankind's religious development primarily in terms of the major age-old and enduring questions that still hide behind differences in theologies and religious practices. The compiling of such a list of mankind's hardest and most serious questions, still only partially answered, is not intended to be taken as an outline of the history of mankind's religious development. It is meant rather to suggest a dynamic way for our examination of these differing beliefs.

Also, as adult leaders who care about children's religious growth, we may find it suggestive to discover, when faced with the children's direct questions, how much these resemble those age-old questions that men began asking thousands of years ago. Even though we and the children will find our own answers differing from those of other people and those of other times, yet, if we sense the emotional experiences and questions beneath the beliefs, we can the more easily feel empathy with those who differ because we recognize our common human needs. It may also relieve us of a need to claim superiority.

Furthermore, in this way we may lessen the need to settle on sure answers for the sake of finding comfort. We may even find, as we come to realize the universality of our major questions, that our sense of human brotherhood will naturally expand and deepen, and even our own desire to continue to question may be given an added incentive.

# What Then Have Been the Enduring Questions Behind Religious Beliefs?

## *The Question of the Beginning of All Beginnings*

Probably no other question has been more universally and continuously asked than this: "How did everything begin?" "In the Beginning"—Who? What? How? Why?

Perhaps *Homo Sapiens* wondered often and asked many questions before this last and most far-reaching one came to his consciousness. We do not know what his very first questions were. There is considerable evidence to show that this question regarding beginnings was among his early ones. Probably no other has had so many imaginative stories woven around it as has this one big question. How did everything begin?

No longer need the children in our Schools of Religion be left exclusively dependent on the two Hebrew creation stories in Genesis of our Bible. Scores of such myths and poems on creation from many different lands have been discovered and translated by archaeologists and anthropologists and made easily available. Out of this recently acquired wealth of material, fifteen creation "myths" have been carefully chosen because of their special dramatic and pictorial appeal to appreciation by boys and girls, and gathered into a book now available for use in Schools of Religion. This book, *Beginnings: Earth, Sky, Life, Death,*[4] in fact, contains not only these fifteen ancient myths, but also the modern scientists' explanations of beginnings, a brief but illustrated account of their great "myth" of evolution and its beginnings.

Futile as some say it is even to ask this question about the first of all beginnings, man seems unable to keep his mind off it. Because he has never ceased striving to trace his history back and back to its very beginnings, man has added steadily to his understanding of himself and of the cosmos in which he found himself living—its composition, its nature, and its ways of continuing change. Hopeless as the search for an ultimate answer may be, the very effort to reach farther and farther back in time has been far from futile. Although the spokesmen for the various religions probably all sensed their inability to find the full answer, they still seem to have felt that there must be some answer. Although they might never grasp it fully, yet they would attempt to utter the mystery through symbols and myths, even as the scientists themselves are continually trying to do.

### The First Answer—God, the Original Creator

The most nearly common and universal element in the answers given to this basic question of the beginning of all beginnings has been expressed by some word for deity. (In English our general word is *God*.)

As man continued to struggle with this question of the original Cause or Creator, and tried to imagine what he or she or it might have been like, his differences in thought became evident. How did the Creator do the creating? Was the Creator both male and female?

Was the Creator like the humans created? How did the Creator himself begin? Was it as a babe, as a seed, as an egg? Did the Creator himself grow? Or was the Creator eternal?

Many of the ancient myths, such as the Genesis myth, begin with an already existing chaos of water and earth. The Chinese pictured the Creator as himself beginning as a dwarf and growing, with his creation, into a giant. The Japanese imagined a small green sprout pushing itself up from the deep. The Greeks imagined a primal egg out of which was hatched the god of love. The Hebrews pictured the Creator as coming down from the sky. The Bushmen imagined him as coming up out of the mysterious darkness under the earth.

Modern astronomers, physicists, and biologists have recently revived their interest in speculation regarding beginnings. Some would say, "In the beginning was hydrogen." Others would venture even further back to a primeval bundle of nuclear elements which were in utter confusion until the tension between them brought the first great explosion, followed by a succession of explosions, producing the organized atoms of hydrogen, then helium, and so on and on until our vast and complex universe evolved.

Since in our liberal Religious Schools children are now reading these myths and scientific speculations, they are being exposed to a variety of conceptions of a primal Creative Divinity. If they are not left wonderingly sensitive to the Mystery and are asking no questions, their studying must be very unimaginatively led, or else they must feel too timid or overwhelmed to question.

### God as Continuing Creator or Creative Process

Although the first humans entered a very old universe, they did not enter a static or completed one. In fact, they found themselves to be but one kind of creature alongside many other kinds, and everything seemed to be moving or changing. They felt aliveness hidden underneath the surface of everything, even as they felt aliveness within themselves. Daily they discovered new living creatures being born; they knew not how. They found new plants pushing up out of the earth. So it was natural, as time passed, that our first ancestors began asking new questions: "Who keeps making the new babies? Who makes the new fruits and flowers?" So the thought of creative power mysteriously acting all about them brought Divinity right into everyday living.

Worship of this "Continuing Creative Principle" has permeated religious ceremonies and thinking from the most primitive times until the present. All the so-called "fertility cults" featured this power of creation. The mysterious act of sexual embrace has been both sensuously enjoyed and also reverenced as the most divine of human powers. In fact, the first human images of gods, thus far discovered, have been images of pregnant women.

Many philosophers today refer to Divinity as the "Continuing Creative Process" permeating reality everywhere. Thus by using an abstract word they avoid the picture of a manlike Divinity, and center thought upon the basic Mystery of the origin of life in all its continuing new forms.

The mystery of creation still hides in the molecule DNA. No other question is more absorbing to biochemists today than this. What is the creative principle that lies apparently within this invisible microscopic bit of protoplasm to be found within every living cell, apparently holding within it half the pattern or code for the creation of a new life?

Some of today's astronomers also are even proposing that the entire cosmos is creatively expanding by the creation of new atoms of hydrogen to replace those that disintegrate. In short they imagine the whole cosmos as a continuing "Creative Process."

As long as mankind is unable to create new life out of inorganic matter, he can scarcely do other than admit that the power to create new life is beyond present human attainment. But is it beyond all natural powers within the cosmos? Did the universe create itself? Or did a Creative Power precede all that men call the natural cosmos? Did a Creative Power wholly other than the "natural" create the natural? That is, was it supernatural? Or has this Creative Power always been natural, being latent within it? To these further questions, different answers have been given.

The word *God* has included both concepts: a Creative Power entering from outside, and a Creative Power that has always been inherent and within. Whether this question is answered in one way or another, the Mystery is not changed or taken away. Some word or group of words is needed to express this Creativity.

## A Second Great Question: Why Death?

*Homo Sapiens* early discovered a contrasting invisible process pervading his world. Not only were new forms of life continually appearing; but there were others that were being destroyed. Not only were new creatures being born, but others were dying. Instinctively every living creature wants to live, yet why this continuous threat of death?

Centuries ago the Hindus placed images of the Destroying Deity alongside the images of the Creator and Preserver of Life. Zoroaster proposed a God of Light and a God of Darkness. Christianity and Judaism both also early assumed two deities, the Good Creator and the Evil One who was the initial Cause of the first coming of death into the world. Western theology has, therefore, pictured human history as a combat between the good and the evil, the Creator and the Destroyer, as long as time lasts. So in trying to find an answer to this large and troublesome question, man again needed to enlarge his thought of Divinity to include both what seemed good and what seemed evil; both life and death.

Some objected to harmonizing these opposites into one Divinity, and as a result imagined two antagonistic gods. Others began asking whether death might not be a blessing after all if one took a long-time look? How could any kind of evolution of species have proceeded without the death of the old?

Even in the inorganic world, modern scientists have discovered a similar alteration between developing organization and developing disintegration. The ancient Chinese decided there were two complementary forces at work, the *Yang* and the *Yin,* and that both were in reality good. So the Taoists found a new way of describing Divinity, not merely as the Creative Force, but as the Way—the Tao—including the full range of processes at work within the Cosmos. To find and to understand the Way—the Tao—is to find God.

In the Western world also, many have felt the need

to broaden their thoughts of God to include all life and all existence, both what seems good and what seems not good, a meaning for everything taken together. So for many, "Universal Nature" is the equivalent for God. This is Deity in John Burrough's terms, "with whom our relation is as intimate as that of a babe in its mother's womb, or the apple on the bough—the God . . . from whom there is no escape."

Such a Deity is natural in the sense that it acts within the limits of the natural cosmos. It is super-human in the sense that it transcends all human powers. It is Deity, hidden as it were in the Ways of Nature, in the so-called "Design of the Universe." It is close to Einstein's thought, "Anyone who has seriously studied science is filled with a conviction that a spirit tremendously superior to the human spirit manifests itself in the law-abidingness of the world, before whom we with our simple powers, must humbly stand back." [5]

## What Is Death? Why Old Age, Sickness, Suffering?

The mystery of suffering and death had a further challenge imbedded within it. Was death the end? In death that elusive living part disappeared. But where? We have strong evidence to show that man began imagining some kind of living after death long before he learned to write his thoughts. The possibility of living on and on gave man rich opportunities for projecting his hopes into the future. The thoughts that resulted added a seriousness to man's short life as being but a destiny-determining preparation for a life beyond all temporal measurement. So men's thoughts of God expanded until Divinity became the determiner of an ultimate destiny beyond time.


## *Are There Better Ways of Living?*
## *Are There Rules to Go By?*

If then human life is so short and hazardous on this earth, yet a part of something so everlasting, how make it mean the most? Are there better ways of living? How could one find them out? Are there any rules to go by?

So more characteristics were added to men's thoughts of Divinity. God must have intended men to obey certain laws. What were these laws? Thus law codes developed. Certain wise men, chiefs, and rulers had them written down and proclaimed. Punishments and rewards were attached to them. Of course, historians today assume that men thought out these laws themselves as a result of their experiences as rulers. But where did their thoughts come from? "Perhaps from the Creator God," said the people of long ago. In any case, as time passed, these laws grew in importance, and God was thought of as a Law Giver, a Punisher, Rewarder, and Judge.

There is much need in life for obedience, and it has always been difficult for man to distinguish between the laws that apparently find their authority in the very nature of Nature, and the laws pertaining to human relations that have been tentatively proclaimed by men in power, sometimes wisely and sometimes unwisely.

Man can never afford to abandon the effort to find the true laws for living. Yet living by laws is not enough. Man's potential nature has within it deeper roots than those that can be touched by laws. Feelings can not be commanded into existence, yet they are the most precious of all experiences. So again man's thoughts of Divinity needed enrichment.

## *What Would a Truly Good Person Be Like?*

Men said: "Show us a really good person and we will try to be like him. We need to watch and come to know a really good person as he lives day by day. We need to understand how he feels, how he thinks, so that we may learn to be like him."

When, therefore, good and compassionate teachers appeared now and then, men flocked to them and tried to understand and follow them. Whether the Creator God had really sent these outstandingly good men into the world or not, there they were. And in a true sense they became other men's spiritual guides. Understanding human weaknesses, they became also man's compassionate saviors. Thus thousands, yes, millions, stretched their thoughts to include these their own human brothers in their thoughts of God. These persons, they said, must be like God. How could the Creator be less than his creatures?

So the word *God* was again enlarged to include within it mankind's highest ideals. If Divinity was not really like such men, there were those who wished that God might be like them, full of patience and love and forgiveness; and they decided to act as if God were an embodiment of these high ideals.

We can be sympathetic toward those who feel strengthened by such beliefs, for we too have felt the uplift that comes when we see our ideals even partially embodied in real persons. We may think it wishful thinking to call these ideals *God*. We may prefer to hold fast to the more impersonal concept of God as the "Creative Process," yet we can still look up to such ideals with hope and purposeful longing, and at the same time examine them critically and realistically.

Then, too, if we remind ourselves that the equating of human ideals with God came as a result of men's yearning after these ideals and their possible exaggerated wish for a final sanction for them, we can at least join in the endeavor to examine the worth of the ideals, help in enlarging and in deepening their meanings rather than deny the ideal hopes.

## *"From Whence Cometh My Help?"*

The higher and more vital the ideals became, the stronger grew the sense of inadequacy for achieving them. So these well-known words of the Psalmist expressed another of humanity's perennial questions. Perhaps it has been the first and most basic of all of them. From the earliest days of man's conscious thoughts, he must have felt his dependency on powers beyond his control. His ignorance was profound. The dangerous exigencies threatening his existence were unremitting. His desire to survive was compelling. He became sensitive to invisible powers. He sensed power, life, and things moving and changing with some regularity and yet with unexpected surprises. His curiosity was kindled. He must find out more. He felt he needed help. Where could he find it? He determined to begin testing his resources. He began to feel he was not alone. He felt there were invisible companions somewhere, of some kind. He would experiment to see if he could find them. He needed help. So praying may have begun. Perhaps first to the dream spirits of those who had died.

Even to this day, prayers come to most of us almost instinctively when we find ourselves face to face with great danger. Our hearts cry out for help of some kind. From whence does our help come? What kind of help? Does our asking for help make any difference?

## God—A Word with a Host of Meanings

Thus the word *God* has symbolized many different meanings. It still does. Each is a partial answer to a question of large importance.

The word *God* has meant the Life-giving Element, the Creative Principle within our cosmos (and perhaps outside as well), from the very beginning to the very end—if there ever was a beginning or ever will be an end.

The word *God* has meant also the destroying principle, which complements the principle of creation and makes possible creative evolution.

The word *God* has stood for the actual processes of all Nature, its laws, its evolution, its goal-seeking ways, its organizations, its disorganizations, its designs and its chances.

The word *God* has stood for that to which man must be obedient, the laws he must obey or die, the knowing of good from evil.

The word *God* has stood for man's ideals, not yet

attained; his hopes of perfection; his dreams of eternity, justice, truth, compassion, and forgiveness.

The word *God* has expressed both the *Alpha* and the *Omega* of life, the beginning and the end, as well as the possible timelessness of all Being.

Indeed, through the word *God* man has tried to gather up all his experiences and to find all the values potentially there.

The word *God* has stood for humanity's effort to organize his philosophy, about his own and all other existences beside, into one unified whole.

No word in the English language holds within it such a host of meanings.

The word alone gives no one right answer, nor even a consistent variety of answers. It does express, however, man's expectation that there are answers and that trying to discern at least some parts of these answers, living by them, testing their worth, and creating new answers when old ones no longer satisfy is supremely worthwhile.

It, therefore, seems of importance to us and to our children to renew our understanding and respect for the many meanings this word *God* has had and still expresses. Let us not be afraid to speak of God, feeling overawed by the imponderable nature of Divinity. Neither let us speak carelessly.

If in full honesty we can still retain the use of the word, high values may be gained, for in so doing we and the children with whom we speak will feel we belong within a community of great personalities, including both many who have lived before us and thousands who are our contemporaries.

If in all honesty we find we can not use the word for some of these values, let us try to find other words that are more fully expressive and use them, lest by becoming silent both we and our children may live life with unnoticing eyes, unaware of the glow in the natural half-hidden Mystery of existence.

This way of dealing with theological ideas, namely, looking at religious beliefs as the natural products of universal emotional and philosophical needs and as the answers to man's hardest and most significant questions, rather than as dogmatic or revealed statements of truth or falsehood, may not be the way to foster the development of aggressive fighters against orthodoxies. It does have its appeal, however, as a promising way of encouraging persons able to acquire intelligent convictions while at the same time developing a breadth of sympathetic understanding. It has proven in experience to be an interesting way to boys and girls because it is a dynamic way of relating religious beliefs to the realities of life. In this way there lies also some hope of developing eventually a world-wide religious community freed from rivalries and antagonisms.

It is my hope that the following illustrations of actual experience with boys and girls in this way of examining differing thoughts of God may at least encourage others to venture.


## Illustrations from Experience

### A Fifth Grade Class Shares Its Questions

Dr. William A. Shimer had been invited by a fifth grade class to meet with them in order to help them answer a number of questions that they had been ask-

ing about God. This experience had been so interesting
to the class that they decided to suggest that Dr. Shimer
be invited to speak to the entire department at the next
regular service of worship. So the boys and girls planned this entire service.

When the meeting opened the next Sunday morning three children were seated on the platform alongside their guest, Dr. Shimer. They had chosen the
songs and the responsive reading. One of them introduced the speaker, and another led in the closing prayer
which a committee of the class prepared beforehand.

John introduced Dr. Shimer by telling of the questions they had been asking, how Dr. Shimer had talked
to them the previous Sunday, and why they had asked
him to come again to speak to the entire department.

When Dr. Shimer rose to speak he held in his hand
a rather large piece of cardboard on which the children
had written seven questions in all. "Of course," he said,
"you do not really expect me to know how to answer.
The best I can do is to tell you how I think about them."
Then he began, taking the questions up one by one.

### Question No. 1. What Does God Look Like?

"What does John look like?" he asked, turning to
the leader of the service. "Could you describe what
John looks like? You can tell what color his eyes are
and the shape of his nose and face, how tall he is, what
kind of clothes he's wearing, but would that really tell
you what John looks like? There are many other things
about John which we could not get at all from just
the way he looks. In fact, the most interesting and im-

portant things we would like to know about John we would not find out by knowing what he looks like.

"If then we are unable to say what John looks like, how can we expect to say what God looks like? And yet perhaps we can tell about as well what God looks like as we can tell what John looks like, for we are looking at God all the time! Whenever we look at anything in the world we are really seeing God; that is, we are seeing God's body, we might say.

"It seems to me that we might call everything in this whole universe God's body, that is, everything that can be seen. We have to guess about what we cannot see in the same way we have to guess about John from what we see. How do we know, for example, that John is alive? You may say he can move, but the Hudson River can move too and yet you would not say it is alive, as John is alive. The reason we think that John is alive is because he seems like us. We *feel* alive, therefore, we think that John must be alive too.

"So it is about God and this universe. The scientists tell us that we are all made out of the same substances. The same energy that is in the things around us, the earth, the sky, is also in our bodies. So we think that God must be something like us. Each one of us then is a small part of God."


Question No. 2. Where Does God Come From?

"This is a question we cannot answer. We can ask where does a stick come from and trace it back and back and back, but we finally come to a place where we cannot answer our question. We think of God as al-

ways being here. We find it hard to imagine a time
when God was not."

### Question No. 3. How Does God Get Into
### Pictures If You Can't See Him?

"You must remember that the pictures that can be
seen now and then of God are merely how some artist
imagined God might look, for no one can see God."

### Question No. 4. If We Can't See God
### How Do We Know Him?

"If you can't see John, how do you know him? It
is the same with God. Each time we find something new
about this universe or about ourselves we are finding
out something about God. For God is everything and
everywhere. So we are really learning more and more
about God as we learn more and more about the world,
and everything around us in it."

### Question No. 5. Does God Make Us Bad
### When We Are Bad?

"Well, since we are part of God, we would have to
say the bad in us is part of God. Let us think of it in
this way. We have inherited from our animal ancestors
the urge to eat sugar. Animals need sugar to give them
strength, so do we. But animals had to hunt hard for
the sugar they ate so ordinarily they did not have much

of it. We, however, because of our science have learned how to turn sugar cane and beets into sugar and sugar into candy. It is so easy for us to find sugar that we are tempted to eat more than we should. When we do this we harm our bodies and so we suffer. We do what is wrong, but the urge to eat the sugar is good because if we did not have it we could not be strong. So it seems to me that when we do not control our appetites we do what is not good and we are bad, but that does not mean that God is bad because what is given us is good."

### Question No. 6. How Did God Come To Be One God?

"We have come to think of God as one God because we have come to believe that this universe is unified. Although we speak of many solar systems, and even of more than one universe, scientists are inclined to think all things put together are really one."

Just then Dr. Shimer dropped the cardboard from which he was reading and it fell to the floor. "What made this cardboard fall when I let it go?" *Gravity* was the answer. "Is gravity only right here in this room? Or is it only here to make us fall if we are trying to go to the top of some building and walk off? No! *Gravity* is something that is everywhere. It is out in the spaces where the stars are. It is pulling all the time, keeping the planets and the moon and the sun all moving around and around. The force of *gravity* seems to be everywhere holding things together, not too far apart and not too close. So we believe that the universe is *one* and if the universe is one, then God is one."

Question No. 7. Why Do We Pray? And Do
Scientists Pray?

"Scientists no longer pray for miracles to happen;
that is, they do not expect the laws of nature to be
changed by their asking God to change them. Yet there
are scientists who still pray. By this they mean that they
are always longing and hoping to understand the universe better for they know we are a part of this great
wonder, that we are able in a measure to change it, and
they want to find out the best ways of changing it. They
think of the whole universe as being one LIFE. They
think they see a great Mind or Spirit working within
the entire universe. We and all other living creatures
are parts of this tremendous Living Energy. If only
we understood more about it and what all the changing is for, then we could decide better how to do our
parts."

On the wall back of the platform, Dr. Shimer had
hung a Japanese painting of Fujiyama, but it was completely covered by a piece of cloth. Dr. Shimer stepped
over in front of the picture and said, "You have been
curious about this painting, haven't you? You have
been wishing I would lift the cover so that you could
see what it is about.

"Now we might say that this painting (if we could
make it unthinkably large) is something like God, or
it is something like the whole of this great wonderful
living universe in which we live and which we are very
small parts of. And if we could imagine this painting as
being *alive*, growing and changing as our bodies grow

and change, then it would seem even more like God.

"We have minds and are curious, even though we are but very small specks or parts in this whole great moving picture. We want to know more about everything, to understand what the universe is becoming, and what we are becoming. We'd like to know how to work with its ways of changing rather than *against* them. We'd like our little parts to make the whole more beautiful rather than to spoil it. If we are having a part in painting such a living picture, we would like to make our parts fit properly into the whole."

Then Dr. Shimer lifted one corner of the cloth. "What do you see? Can you guess what the painting is about?" The children were too puzzled at first to guess. He lifted another corner. Then little by little he revealed more and more of the painting, until finally he threw the cloth away and the whole beautiful painting was visible. The interest was intense.

"You might say you have been praying as the scientists pray. They do not ask that the universe be changed to suit their desires. They want to understand more and more of it, so that they can live and work with it. As the picture grows they want their own small parts to grow in harmony with it. None of us, not even the scientists, probably will ever know what it is all about. We may never know God wholly, but we keep on trying to find out more and more. As we understand more, here a little, there a little, then we will understand ourselves better. We will know better how to live out our own little parts. This kind of praying, such as the scientists do, I think we will want to keep on trying to do as long as we live."

Closing Prayer [Composed by a committee of the class, John leading.]

O God, we boys and girls have been trying to learn about you. There are many things we do not understand but we are finding out some things. We are glad we can go on learning about you as long as we live.

We thank you for the energy and power which is everywhere and in everything. Energy is in the sunshine and the rain. It is in the chlorophyll which makes earth and water and sunshine into food for men and animals. Energy is in people. It makes them able to work, to do all kinds of labor.

Forgive us when we use our energy to harm and not to help. Forgive us when we waste it by losing our tempers and being cross, by teasing our brothers and sisters, by quarreling and fighting. Forgive us when we waste our energy in cheating or telling lies. Help us to learn good ways to use our energy.

O God, there are many things we would like to pray for. Help us to find answers to the questions we are asking. Help us to learn to stop and think. Help us to find better ways of living together so we won't have wars. Amen.


Children's Comments After the Service

Some of the children's remarks afterwards show how deeply Dr. Shimer's talk sunk in.

"Oh boy, wasn't that good! It cleared up a lot of things for me."

"But wasn't it tantalizing!"

"That man certainly knows how to explain things."

[*Dr. William A. Shimer, the speaker, was at the time editor of* The American Scholar. *He is the author of* Conscious Clay. (*New York: Scribners, 1948*). *In this book he has elaborated the religious philosophy he attempted to explain to the children.*]

## Ways of Imagining God: The Children's Ways and the Ways of Others

Since in two classes in the Junior Department the children had been painting their own ideas and feelings about God, this meeting was planned to give recognition to their imaginative thoughtfulness, and to encourage further meditation by all the children of the department.

In preparation, six of the children's paintings were collected with the children's permission, and placed over one another on an easel at the center of the platform. In addition an opaque projector, capable of projecting printed pictures from books and magazines upon a screen, was set in readiness for use and the screen was hung.

An appropriate opening song was sung and the entire group joined in a responsive reading of selections chosen from several different scriptures (mimeographed copies having been inserted in our homemade song and reading book).

Then I explained the experiences of two of the classes, out of which our morning's program had grown. I told how I had discovered that some of the boys and girls in two classes had been painting pictures of their thoughts and feelings about God. Of course, they are not meant to be pictures of God, I told them, for God is invisible. All that anyone can put down on paper is something that suggests just a little of how he thinks and feels about God. When I found out how much thinking these boys and girls had put into their paintings, I asked them if they would be willing to show them to you all, and if they would tell you what they were trying to say about God.

Six paintings in all were shown. The following descriptions are given as nearly in the children's own words as the teacher's reports permit.

1. This is a painting of one great eye because God is one who knows everything that is happening all the time everywhere.

2. I wanted to show that God is very old. He must be old if he was in the beginning before the world was made. So I have painted him with a long beard, flying through the clouds, where he can look down on all people and things. In one hand he is carrying a dark ball which is the Night, and in the other hand he is carrying a light yellow ball which is the Day.

3. This is a painting of a stream of light with different sunbeam colors in it. It streams down from high up onto houses and people on earth. The different colors are like different parts of God. Sometimes God seems like dark red and purple, and sometimes God seems like soft blue, and sometimes God seems bright like yellow.

4. This is another painting of God flying through the sky. I wanted especially to make God's face look kind. The yellow jacket I painted on God stands for sunshine, the green shorts are for all green growing things, and the trailing scarf of blue is for the sky, and the red wings are for power.

5. God seems to me like the sun. So I have painted this big red sun with rainbow colors around it in the center of my painting. Below are many birds, and some animals and green plants and trees. God is for all people and animals and birds and growing things. (This boy was an expert on birds, and they were very prominent in his painting.)

6. This is a painting of a large crown high in the center. Below are a large boat, an airplane and a scientist working with a test tube in his laboratory. This shows that God is greater than all the ships in the world and all the airplanes and all that the scientists can find out. God is wider than the widest sea, greater than the greatest invention, and more wonderful than the greatest scientists.

The interest of the entire group was very keen throughout. We might well have spent time in talking about these paintings and in gathering other thoughts from the other children and to have ended the meeting with a prayer or song or both. Then the following Sunday I could have shown the pictures through the projector.

Instead, by means of the opaque projector, I threw on the screen a number of photographs of paintings and sculptured images of God's form as imagined by people of different lands and times. These I had cut out of old magazines or traced from books. Altogether they represented Divinity in a number of different forms.

There were gods in animal shapes, such as Hathor, the Sacred Cow of ancient Egypt; the Golden Bull of Babylonia (imagined as in the crescent moon). There was also the swift flying Hawk, again from Egypt, and

the Dragon from China (imagined as being in the moving clouds).

There were also pictures portraying gods in human form, for example, the storm God of Canaan holding a thunderbolt in his hand; the Creator God Shiva
of India and his wife Kali, the Destroyer God. There
was also a picture of Indra, the king of heaven, having eyes all over his strong body. There was also a picture of the ancient Mother Goddess of the Middle East,
and the great Goddess of Mercy, Kwannon of China,
who had a thousand arms with which to embrace all her
children.

We showed also pictures of God as seen in the best
and noblest of men, such as pictures of Jesus, Buddha,
and Confucius. There was also Akhenaten's unusual
picture of Deity as the radiant Sun sending its life-giving arms of sunshine all around, touching every creature
with the gift of life. We showed also two pictures from
Michelangelo, showing God creating the birds and fish,
and also swinging the world around.

Altogether the total experience was an awakening
one for all of us. By putting the artistic attempts preserved for us from the past alongside the children's own
efforts we heightened their appreciation of their own
work by imparting to them the feeling of having attempted, without knowing it, what some of humanity's
greatest artists have tried to do again and again. Each
depicting in his own picture or statue some element in
his thought of God that was original and somewhat
different from the others.

### Life Long Ago, Today, and Tomorrow
### (A Pictorial Portrayal of the Story of Evolution)

A class of ten-year-olds took full responsibility for this service of worship. On the platform they had placed their own handmade kind of moving picture frame. On two rollers fastened upright on a strong base was wrapped a long scroll, on which were pasted a series of the children's own paintings. They were large and colorful so that all the audience could see them.

In addition, two of the class held a very long time-line. On a scale of one inch to a million years they had marked off the ages in the evolutionary process. One by one, each of the eleven pictures was described by some member of the class. The descriptions were simply worded, and either read by the children or spoken from memory.

They began with a picture of a lifeless, barren, rocky world and an empty sea.

Next the sea was shown covered with green scum made by millions of living, unicellular green algae in the water.

Next came the unicellular algae that became the first animals, the ones who had to eat the green algae to survive since they had lost their own power to create chlorophyll directly from the sunshine. This stage was represented principally by amoebae which the children themselves had drawn after examining them through a good microscope.

Next were the pictures of the first multicellular animals and plants; then the first animals that ate other

animals, and that had developed various kinds of shells
for protection, some having sharp points and horns and
some having poisoned bristles.

Next came the animals with their bony structures
on the inside, the animals having backbones.

After these came the first amphibians who dared
to venture to live part of the time on land.

Then came the real land animals, the mammals described as dog-like creatures with four feet.

After the mammals came the birds, those who ventured to fly.

Then the first apelike humans, and last men like
those of today. These were represented by a picture of
New York City.

All the time during the showing of this series of
drawings, two other members of the class were standing
at the side of the platform holding between them the
time-line. After the showing of each picture these
children unfolded the time-line far enough to represent
the number of millions of years it took to make that
much progress. As the ages were unrolled the line grew
longer and longer, until it reached all the way around
one side of the room and halfway across the back. The
unrolling of this time-line was of very keen interest to
all the children. When at the end, the age of man was
unrolled it was but *one inch long!*

There was still a space on the moving picture roller
that had not been shown. This was now unrolled. It
was marked "Life Tomorrow," but no picture had been
drawn on it. The speaker who showed it told why it
was left blank, and read the following statement the
class had made expressing their wishes and hopes regarding the future:

The last picture we have left blank. We wish we could come back to the world after a thousand years and see it. We would like to find everybody with good homes, enough food and clothing and money. We would like it if there could be kindness and justice for everybody. We would like all children to be able to stay in their homes, and for fathers and mothers always to be together. The greatest wish of all is for no more wars, but for peace everywhere.

The supervisor of the department said this had been a real prayer. Then the meeting was closed.

[*Summary of a record written by Elsie M. Bush, teacher of a fifth grade class in the Riverside Church School, New York City, April 2, 1939.*]

# CHAPTER FIVE

# How Then Can We Still Pray?

"I say no man has ever yet been half devout enough;
None has ever yet adored or worshipped half enough;

.    .    .

The wonder is, always and always, how there can be a mean
man or an infidel."

WALT WHITMAN [1]

Perhaps there is no responsibility involved in leading religious gatherings that seems so difficult as leading a group of boys and girls in prayer. This is especially true for those of us whose feelings and thoughts regarding Divinity have been changing, and whose revised faith and theology are still largely inarticulate. It would be simpler to delete praying entirely from such meetings. Yet to do so, without substituting something that encourages a similar emotional outreach seems like cutting out the very heart.

I have been in religious meetings with children when no spoken words of prayer seemed needed. Our feelings were already stirring at unusual depths. Sometimes these feelings seemed satisfyingly expressed in the singing of an appropriately prayerful song. Sometimes a moment of silence meant more than words could have done. More often, however, I felt that the dynamic mood that was developing among the children, because of the story told, or the talk given, or the discussion participated in, needed some brief verbal expression by the leader to enrich and strengthen it. Such experiences led me usually to speak a prayer after the story or talk and before the closing song. I confess, however, it has never been easy.

At such times, I have felt it important to shun all impression of seeming to moralize through the prayer, but rather to try to express, as far as it was humanly possible, such a prayer as each child might perhaps truly wish himself to pray and in which I could in all sincerity also join as expressing my own yearnings or feelings or purposes. For a leader at such a time to stand apart from the group, as it were, and to pray *for* them rather than *with* them may well put out the vital spark in the experience of prayer. The feeling that the leader and the group are sincerely united in thoughtful fellowship is beyond all mere devices and techniques. Especially with these pre-adolescent children who are reaching out so eagerly for independence, any touch of moralizing may stunt their spontaneous emotional fervor.

This caution, however, touches but the surface of our problem. For many of us our private praying is no longer the regular ritual it used to be. Our substitutes are informal, unarticulated times and moments without a name. We still take time out now and then, if not regularly, for quiet contemplation. We react spontaneously to immediate experiences, with exhilaration or reverence, or with feelings of being enveloped in the Mysterious Wonder of being. We experience also times of weakness, helplessness, and despair, when we yearn for a Great Friend to encourage us, for greater strength than our own to empower us. Now and again we are overcome with our sorry feelings of guilt, and our yearning for compassion and forgiveness. We even set aside times for self-examination, digging into our motivations, and pulling out of our unconscious our rejected memories until we find our nakedness uncovered and we feel healthy once more. We still even have times when to live seems richly good so that we feel like singing "a joyful song unto the Lord" even though we may no longer know how to imagine "the Lord."

We still know many such experiences, perhaps we have them more often than we did when we prayed regularly, yet we have lost our name for them. They come to us usually unsolicited and unexpectedly; we so seldom plan for them. We do not usually articulate our feelings in words that seem like prayers, nor are they linked with "religious" places and settings.

In leading services of worship, however, a leader is never alone. We have a responsibility for trying to express the feelings of all who have gathered together. They have grown accustomed to certain forms. Even the simple bowing of the head, the closing of the eyes to external sights, and the simple words, "Let us unite in prayer," seem to induce feelings of reverence. But what words can we use? How can we develop the ability to be sensitive to the sincere feelings of those beside us? And how much can we express with full sincerity?

## Praying Without Petitioning

Prayer is another of those long-used words that has had many different meanings. Whether the word itself be discarded or retained is not the important issue. Again we need to reach beneath the forms and rituals

to find the intimate psychological experiences that praying has expressed. Which of these types of experiences
are still valuable for us in an age of science? And which
tend to destroy our mental and emotional integrity?

First of all let us examine a few of the meanings
for prayer which seem clearly unjustifiable and a real
hindrance to the development of spiritual or psychological health. Perhaps the most common meaning of
all is the thought of prayer as bringing a kind of magic
power that can be obtained through the saying of some
specific set of words or simply by asking God for help.
That some of the children in our Junior Department
had been given this impression is clearly shown in the
panel discussion they had among themselves on *"How
We Feel Ourselves Inside of Us"* (p. 149). This impression is probably not intentionally conveyed by parents;
nevertheless, when children at a very early age are taught
to pray and these prayers consist in the main of petitions
for special kinds of blessings, the conclusion that some
kind of magic has been accomplished seems natural.

The second misconception regarding prayer which
seems a hindrance is the idea that in order to pray a person must be able to imagine a supernatural personal
God to whom he addresses his prayer. Otherwise it is
assumed that prayers have to be addressed to emptiness,
and are, therefore, wholly futile. Because of this
thought of prayer, thousands of people believe that
they can never again pray.

This seems to me to be based upon two unneeded
and undesirable suppositions. First, that through prayer
one is able to reach outside the natural universe into a
supernatural realm, and thereby gain an increment of
supernatural power. Second, that by doing so one can

overcome the restrictions to power involved in our finite nature; in short, that we can reach out for a power that can break natural laws. The scientists to whom the children wrote made it clear in their responses that they could no longer think of prayer as giving the power to transcend natural laws. So also did their minister. This thought involved for the children a drastic rethinking of prayer. In this they were probably not far behind many adults.

When adults contemplate asking God to send rain or to prosper their business ventures, many are likely to refrain. On the other hand, even the astronauts have been known to put a St. Christopher medal in their capsule, and soldiers have often carried copies of the Bible in their uniform pockets to protect them from the fatal bullet.

There is a very fundamental reconceiving of the purposes of prayer which is needed by our generation if it is to be intellectually and emotionally whole. Since we understand the laws of psychological development less well than we understand the laws of the physical world, and since we believe that in this area there is more room for creativity, we seem to feel freer to ask God to "bring peace on the earth," or "to change the hearts of men," than we do to ask God directly for food and money.

Yet even these expressions in our prayers need re-examination. Perhaps we can learn something from the East in this regard. It is said that Mahatma Gandhi never spoke petitionary prayers, and seldom spoke of Divinity. Yet he had his own daily prayer that he repeated to himself as he meditated, to remind him of the great principles to which he had committed his whole being.

> "I will be truthful.
> I will suffer no injustice.
> I will be free from fear.
> I will not use force.
> I will be of good-will to all men." [2]

In contrast to petitionary prayers let us gather in our thought some of the other varieties of experience that have proven to be valuable, and have been expressed in prayer:

Times for quiet and serious meditation, with as many of the barriers to straight thinking removed as one is capable of relinquishing.

Times when we feel at peace and thankful, counting blessings one by one.

Times when life's baffling tragedies overwhelm us and our sympathies bleed and we yearn for comfort.

Times when we are depressed, with feelings of guilt and remorse and we yearn for compassion and forgiveness.

Times when we renew our resolves. We commit ourselves with renewed vigor and faith to unachieved goals.

Times when we feel we are touching the hidden and mysterious, in simple concrete things and persons, or in immeasurably vast phenomena as well.

Times when we feel a mystic union with *The All,* a kind of universalized all—enveloping—inexpressible—great Life.

Times when we want to see ourselves in all our spiritual nakedness, when we yearn to understand and to be made whole.

"Search me, O God, and know my heart.
 Try me and know my thoughts
 And see if there be any wicked way in me."

Psalm 139: 23,24

This prayer of the psalmist preceded his petition: "And lead me in the way everlasting."

In our time, however, the psychiatrists have discovered that searching the heart and knowing the mind call for difficult self-analysis and self-understanding. Some of us need the skilled help of psychiatrists. Yet, in the end, no one can place the responsibility either with the psychiatrist or with the Creator for doing it for us. We must, in reality, learn this self-examining for ourselves if it is to be done.

If we can learn how to discipline ourselves daily by having such times for meditation, self-examination and appreciative gratitude; and if we can help our growing children to begin having them also, we may find, I believe, that when we are gathered together with others in our religious meetings, our meditations together (whether in silence or expressed in words, song, or music) will grow in significance. I can see the possibility of such experiences exceeding in emotional warmth most of the ancient ritualistic forms of routine, communal praying. With children, we have a peculiar opportunity to begin new patterns of praying.

## No One Is Ever Alone

For some of us it may be more fruitful to abandon (for a time at least) the thought of addressing and asking

God for help and to think of praying as conversations primarily with our inner selves. In debating among ourselves whether we pray to ourselves or pray to God, we may be missing the really valuable experience.

Bernard Shaw, in his dramatic version of the story of Joan of Arc, pictures King Charles as chiding her for thinking she had heard voices. "You are simply hearing your own thoughts," he declared. Joan's prompt response was, "Yes, but that's the way God talks to us." No person in this age, knowing what we think we know of the universes and of ourselves, can believe he is utterly alone or utterly outcast or uncared for. There is some thing or some Life other than one's self to commune with. It may be "Nature in its varied forms." It may be what Dr. Tillich calls "the Ground of Being" or it may be what, metaphorically speaking, is more often called "the All Father." Blessed are those who are not afraid to try to both grow in understanding of the self and to learn to achieve deeper understanding of other selves and possibly of a Universal Self. Perhaps this need to escape the sense of isolation and insignificance is the basic need that the practice of times for praying can meet.

# Knowing Something of Mankind's Long Experiences in Prayer

A human phenomenon so nearly universal and so long lasting as praying cannot be intelligently discarded without first learning something of its significance in man's cultural evolution. Whether or not in any particular Church or Religious School, the adult leaders call themselves "Humanists" or "Theists" I believe they should encourage the children to study sympathetically man's experiences in praying. For the sake of their own religious growth, they should first have their own horizons of understanding broadened. Our own world is in need of those who do not merely *admit* intellectually that all humans are of one family; but we need even more those who also *feel* they belong in one brotherhood, having first discovered in themselves some of the emotional needs, fears, and hopes shared universally.

If the classroom discussions grip the children at all vitally, questions about prayer are almost sure to arise at some time during these middle years. These call for serious unhurried consideration. When they are asked, it may be wise to interrupt the general area of study for a period of weeks in order to examine praying through the ages and in different lands. To spend six weeks in studying prayer because it has been put into the curriculum, and to spend six weeks studying prayer because the boys and girls themselves have really become serious about wanting to know what it can all be about, are two entirely different ventures. The first might well be almost lifeless. The second might become an unforgettable venture such as was the case with one sixth grade class some years ago.

## A Little Formality and Ritual

Since sincere, conscious prayer or meditation is sometimes difficult, being an attempt to communicate meaningfully with the invisible self and with invisible and intangible realities surrounding the self, we need at times the help of a few special external forms. The varieties in these repeated forms or rituals have been innumerable, and they have changed with man's growing intelligence. Yet most religious groups still have at least some small quota of religious formalities. These help those who are participating to feel a meaning in just what is being attempted. In our liberal religious societies, we have tended to reduce these rituals to a near minimum in our effort to maintain original and natural emotional reactions to life's experiences. Yet most of us continue to find that some repetitions of dignified and carefully chosen words and forms of behavior are emotionally gratifying as long as we feel true and can speak or sing the words with sincere thoughtfulness.

If I had the opportunity to try again, I would try to be more articulate, honest, and imaginative myself, and would encourage more original expressions from the children.

Following the illustrations from experience for this chapter are a few samples of written words, revealing some of our own efforts to express our prayerful feelings and thoughts in poetry, songs, and responsive readings. These are offered with the hope that they will encourage other children and leaders to feel free to create their own ways of expressing their own true experiences.

## Illustrations from Experience

*Two Months of Asking Question and Looking for Answers with a Sixth Grade Class of Boys and Girls*

Our class had been trying to study about Moses, but for some reason the interest lagged. Finally one morning four of the boys in the class became so unruly that I was desperate and decided not to allow them to go to the departmental service of worship with the rest of the class. I knew the boys were discontented and I was determined to find out what was the matter.

When alone with them, I expressed my irritation and pointed out that what they were doing was getting them nowhere, and that it was spoiling the morning for all the rest. "You might really have a good time studying about religion," I said, "if you got down to business and worked on it." The boys seemed tongue-tied. Finally one of them remarked glumly, "Well, I'd like to know what religion is anyway."

There was a brief discussion about this before I got a piece of paper and asked each one in turn to say what he thought religion was.

Their answers were as follows:

Religion is a feeling people have towards some kind of support.

Religion is worship, prayer, and sacrifice and loving.

Religion is believing in God or in gods or in spirits or superstitions.

Religion is cooperation between God and man.

All were thoughtfully given but, as one would expect, vague. I asked, "Does your thinking about religion make you want to ask any questions?" Then their answers began coming easily. These are the ones I was able to write on the blackboard.

Do scientists pray? Do most of them? Or only a few? Why do they pray?

Why do people go to church?

When we are older will we want to go to church? Why?

Why do people have the feeling of religion?

Some people are afraid to die. Why?

May we go to church sometime?

May we study about these questions?

When the girls returned from the service of worship they were surprised to find these questions on the board. I explained what the boys had been talking about, and that they had made this list of things they were wondering about.

"We made one too, the Sunday the boys were absent, you remember?" said Winifred. "Let's put all our questions together and try to find answers." We all agreed. The girls expressed especially their wish to go to church, too. "Can't we go next Sunday?"

These experiences seemed to show that a study of the children's own questions and ideas of God might be more valuable than to go on with a study of Moses at present.

## Second Sunday

When the children arrived they found written on the blackboard a suggested program for the morning in outline, and a list of several of the questions they had asked the preceding Sunday.

Since they had come expecting to go to church at eleven o'clock, I gave each one of them a church program to look at. We spent about an hour talking over the various parts of the service.

"Why have an organ prelude?" Phyllis asked.

"To make a feeling of reverence," someone said.

"What is reverence?" I asked.

This called forth an unexpectedly varied and rich number of answers beginning with "It's like quiet and beauty and the way you feel in church."

"It's not only in church," said William.

"Where else might you feel reverent, feel quiet and beauty?"

More than a dozen different places in the out-of-doors were mentioned, in addition to the music and quiet, and the stained glass windows, and pieces of art found in the church.

Then I returned to our last week's discussion once more.

"Four of the boys talked about religion last Sunday while you girls were at the service of worship," I said. I read aloud their statements as I had written them down. The girls listened most attentively and seemed impressed that the boys had said so much. I asked if there were any other things that any of them had been thinking about that we might include.

"Well," said Harry. "I'd like to know how religion was found? How was it discovered?" Harry added, "How did religion start anyway?"

"Oh, I know about that," said Phyllis, and she went on to explain about the religion of the cavemen and how that developed into the religion of the Egyptians and the Hebrews many years later. Others in the class helped fill in details from time to time. An excellent summary was made.

"You have asked hard questions," I said, referring to the blackboard again. "How are we going to answer a question like this one: Do scientists pray?"

"Ask a scientist," several said.

"Do you know any?"

"Sure, there's Einstein and Edison—and—."

I remarked that Edison was dead and Einstein might not be in this country right now. "But there are other eminent scientists not so very far away to whom we might write, or perhaps we could ask some of them personally."

The children were very enthusiastic. A number of names were put on the blackboard.

Then we adjourned to go to church. They seemed to be interested throughout the entire service, sat quietly, sang the hymns, whispered an occasional question to me, and jotted others down on pieces of paper.


Third Sunday


I came this morning with a list of the names of twelve prominent scientists with their addresses. The children on their own initiative brought the names of three more. So there was a rich opportunity for personal choice.

First we talked over together the important things to say in our letters. Each one set to work composing his own letter to the man of his choice. Then later each letter was copied in ink on the church stationery and the envelopes addressed and marked "personal."

What time was left over before the departmental service of worship at 11:50 was spent in talking over their feelings and thoughts about the church service they had attended the previous Sunday. More questions were naturally added to the list we already had.

### Fourth Sunday

The children came wondering if any answers from the scientists had arrived at the church office, and were temporarily disappointed that none had been received. So when we gathered together to talk as a class, I asked for ideas on what we might do as we waited for the letters. I made several suggestions. The discussion began to ramble. The children expressed a variety of opinions about prayer. "If you pray you feel better." "People have always prayed to get courage." "Well, how do you know there is a God, anyhow?" Then there was a pause. I felt a need to help them organize their thoughts around a few more tangible experiences.

"People have prayed ever since the time of the cavemen," I said. "Since it is not easy to pray, people have used different things to help them. Can you think of some of the things they have used to help them?"

A number of the members of the class had already been introduced to stories of primitive peoples in

Europe, Africa, and Asia, so their responses came thick and fast. Drums; rattles; prayer wheels; kites in China; horns in India and Palestine; eggs at Easter, flags, bread, and wine among Christians. The Moslems kiss the sacred Mecca stone. People have fasted and counted their prayers on long strings of beads. They wrote their prayers on scrolls of parchment. They danced their prayers and wore masks and skins in order to feel more like the gods. As the listing began to slow down, I suggested the following general plan for what we might be doing ourselves until the answers from the scientists came.

I wrote on the blackboard the words *A Study of Prayer,* and then listed the following:

1. What things have people used to help them pray?
2. What kinds of places have they chosen as special places for praying?
3. What have people been called who have been chosen to help people pray? What do they do?
4. For what have people prayed?
5. How can prayer help us?

I asked if they thought this would be a sensible way to go on with our study. They were enthusiastic and seemed to appreciate having an outline.

From then on we were never at a loss for something interesting to do. I collected illustrated magazines and books and brought them to class. The children, too, brought pictures they found. Some of these were copied. Some were cut out and pasted in our class notebook, and there were many original paintings and drawings made from time to time by individuals. The original paintings of places where they themselves had once felt like praying were the most impressive.

Micky, who occasionally had difficulty working with others around him, went off to another room by himself and came back with an original painting marked *The Path of the Anshents*. By symbols he had represented four religions, those of China, India, Palestine, and Egypt, with arrows pointing to each but all coming from a single central path.

At one point Harry got out the Bible explaining that there were many good things in it, "and they are connected with our study, too." He thought everyone should learn some of the verses.

Phyllis made an original painting. Her own explanation of it was this:

There are three hills, and the highest and the hardest to get to is where the *understanding of religion* is. A misty cloud covers the top. The sun has a cloud over it so that the people can not see it clearly. The sun is religion as a whole. The people climbing this mountain are a Crusader, a Chinese priest, a Russian peasant, and a small child. All are trying to climb the mountain that is the hardest to climb. They wonder if they will ever reach the top.

The Sunday the First Letters
from the Scientists Came

It was a memorable Sunday when three replies to the letters the children had written were waiting. Ruth was surprised when she opened Einstein's to find he had written his in German. Since none of us could read it, Ruth wandered into several classrooms in search of an interpreter. When she returned with a young man teaching a fourth grade class the children listened absorbed as he slowly read the full letter in English.

Later replies came from all the other scientists. We quote three from among them, since they reveal the three slightly divergent points of view represented. All the responses were positive and kindly in their emotional tone. All admitted some kind of praying.

Dear Phyllis,

I have tried to answer your question as simply as possible. Here is my answer.

Scientific research work has as a basis the assumption that all events, including the activities of people, are determined by laws of nature. Therefore, a research worker would hardly be inclined to believe that events could be influenced by prayer; that is, through an expressed wish to a supernatural being.

To be sure, it must be granted that our actual understanding of these laws is only an imperfect framework, so in the last analysis the belief in the existence of these fundamental laws rests also upon a kind of faith. This faith has always been further justified through the achievements of science.

On the other hand, anyone who has seriously studied science is filled with the conviction that a spirit tremendously superior to the human spirit manifests itself in the law-abidingness of the world, before which we with our simple powers must humbly stand. So, the study of science leads to religious feeling, which is certainly to be distinguished from the religiousness of less informed people.

> Friendly greetings to you,
> Yours,
> (signed) A. EINSTEIN

Dear Master Micky Semenoff:

In my mind prayer can be accomplished in various ways. A reverent thought in witnessing some wonder of Nature, some beautiful and natural thing, and the realiza-

tion that I may enjoy it or be governed by it, seems to me
a prayer of thanksgiving—an acknowledgment to the Great
Guiding Spirit of the world in which we live. I often pray
thus—consciously or unconsciously.

                    Sincerely yours,
                    (signed) RAYMOND L. DITMARS

Dear Barbara:

On returning home from abroad, I have just found
your letter asking about my prayer habits. Yes, I do pray,
and frequently, though rarely in a formal manner. My
formal prayer is chiefly confined to church, and the saying
of grace at table, which for me is a real prayer. But I have
long been accustomed to feel that God is always with me
as a companion, knowing my thoughts and actions, an
unseen Friend. With this attitude it is unnecessary to make
a formal prayer; the attitude of referring problems and
needs to this Friend, and of sharing with Him the joy of
living, is a natural one. I find myself greatly comforted
and encouraged by this feeling of His presence.

Perhaps this is the best answer I can give. I hope you
may find the same feeling of His presence.

                    Yours sincerely,
                    (signed) ARTHUR H. COMPTON


The morning Dr. Compton's letter came, the children as they arrived one by one were given it to read.
When everyone had read it, I asked what they thought
about it.

Phyllis said, "He feels more the way I do." Others
echoed her thought. "Yes, it is easier to understand him
than Einstein." I asked, "What is the difference between his point of view and that of Einstein and Dit-
mars?"

Harry answered, "Dr. Einstein thought God was more superior, and Compton thinks God is like a friend."

Barbara said, "Well, you don't hear about law in his letter. It's more personal."

From these comments one senses the children's thoughtful struggling with big ideas and feelings. Even the scientists differed. There was no shortcut to certainty. Yet the children felt themselves growing. They had found a new kind of inner satisfaction. They felt they knew more than they had ever known before. They needed but a little suggestion to set them working out a plan so that they might let the other children in the department know something of what had been happening to them.

They decided to be responsible for a departmental service of worship the following Sunday. The class worked out together the major elements in the plan, and then through some extra meetings and one rehearsal in the assembly room the next Sunday morning they were able to give a simple but impressive dramatic scene, primarily between a father and his son with two girls appearing near the end. Everyone in the class had some special responsibility to carry out, since there were curtains and lights to manage, simple scenery to set, an opaque projector to run; and a leader was needed for the whole service to announce the songs and to lead in a final prayer.

The Dramatic Scene:
A Son Asks Questions of His Father

As the curtains open, the father is sitting at his desk on the right stage. An empty easy chair stands on the opposite side. On an easel in the center, a little back on the stage, is a painting (one of the children's original ones) of a lovely lake cupped within a circle of green hills.

The son enters and approaches his father.

SON. Father, have you got a few minutes to spare?
FATHER. Why sure, son.
SON. Well, Father, I've been wondering a lot about praying. Do people have to pray only in church?
FATHER. Why no, son, I'm sure they don't. Why just look at this painting. [*He steps over to the easel.*] Surely, a person might feel like praying in a beautiful place like this.

Then the father pulled out a drawer of his desk and brought out the paintings the children had made of the places where they had felt like praying. He put them one by one on the easel and commented on them.

The first was of a boy on top of a ski jump, of which he commented, "This boy is about to do a hard thing. It helps him to feel stronger and more able to jump if he prays." Other pictures followed: peasants stopping their work to watch a sunset, a group of boys around a camp fire, a few people looking up at the Aurora Borealis, a boy about to dive into a lake.

After showing all these original paintings by the children, the father turned to another group of pictures which the children had cut out of magazines, showing special places and buildings which people had chosen as places for prayer. These were thrown on a screen by means of the opaque projector. They included mosques in Africa, Persia, and Turkey; a pagoda in Shanghai; a Buddhist temple in Singapore; and several churches in England and America.

Still interested, the son asked for more. So the father showed pictures of the things that people had used to help them pray: a picture of a bell-ringer in a temple in Peking, a Tibetan priest holding a prayer drum, a Japanese priest blowing through a great shell as if it were a trumpet, another priest praying with a rosary, pictures of different shrines, and a statue of Mary with the Christ child.

As the father and son were talking, two girls entered and stood for a while watching and listening. Finally, one spoke up and said that they too had been studying about prayer. One had a painting in her hand. It was the one that Phyllis had painted of the highest and hardest mountain to climb, with the four men who were part way up. Barbara explained its meaning.

Shortly after this, the scene closed when the son said, "Well, I think I understand more about praying now. I thank you all for helping me."

*[This account consists in the main of selections from the reports written weekly by the teacher, Miss Emily Ellis, as part of her regular responsibility to the Church School of the Riverside Church, New York City, 1936.]*

*An Afternoon Meeting With the Senior Minister*

About twenty-five of us gathered in one of the rooms of the church at four o'clock on a Friday afternoon. Dr. Fosdick said that he had no speech to make, but understood that we had some questions which we wished to ask.

HARRY. Dr. Fosdick, we wrote letters to some scientists and asked them whether they prayed and what they prayed for and we got some answers. They all said about the same thing. We thought you might explain better to us what they mean.

DR. FOSDICK. Well, I saw the letters you got and I think they were very nice and friendly. These scientists, some of them I know, some of them are friends of mine. It seems to me that what they are saying is that this universe is controlled by what we call laws, and they do not think that prayer means the breaking of these laws.

It seems to me that laws of nature are not things that bind us but things that help us. If we know the laws of nature and live according to them we have much more power to do things than if we do not know them and do not work with them.

[*He illustrated this by showing how men were able to bridge the Hudson because they understood exactly the laws of gravity and worked with them.*]

Now our minds work according to law as well as things in nature. The more we know about the laws of thinking, the better we can think.

Prayer seems to me one way of working *with* these laws of our inner life. In prayer we fulfill the conditions for a good life. For example, if we are quiet and stop to think without hurry, we think better than if we are in the midst of confusion. If we stop and look at ourselves honestly, if we get down inside ourselves and look at ourselves and then try to be our best and ask God to help us, that is real prayer.

PHYLLIS. Dr. Fosdick, if you take away the miracles from Jesus' life and you just have a teacher who said things but didn't do anything, do you think that people would believe he is as important as they now think he is.

DR. FOSDICK. That is a question that has bothered a good many people. To understand the miracles we need to remember that in the times when Jesus lived, people looked at anything they could not understand as a miracle. Suppose we think of the story of Jesus' walking on the water. Now I do not think that Jesus ever really did that. I cannot imagine the law of gravity being broken so that his body, heavier than water, could walk on it. I can imagine that a sudden storm came up over the Lake of Galilee and as suddenly died down, and that what really happened was that Jesus was calm while the others were frightened.

When you think of some of the stories of healing that are given in the Bible, I can well imagine that some wonderful healings took place. Dr. Carrel, one of these scientists that is a good friend of mine, has just written a book telling how healings are still taking place at Lourdes and at other springs, healings which doctors can not yet explain. But I do not think that any law of nature was broken.

These miracle stories about Jesus do not make Jesus seem any greater. Jesus himself said, "Be quiet

about these healings. Don't talk about them. I do not
want to be known by them." Without the miracles we
have Jesus as a great character, a friend, an ideal. That
is what is important.

PHYLLIS. Dr. Fosdick, do you think that when the
monks were teaching the Indians about Jesus, if they
had not said anything about the miracles of Jesus, and
had just told the Indians about a great teacher, would
the Indians have been converted as quickly as they were?

DR. FOSDICK. I don't know about that, but I think
that it is a mistake to put emphasis on his miracles. His
real greatness lies in his character and his teachings.

[*Dr. Fosdick then told of some extraordinary miracles
which had been related about St. Francis Xavier.*]

VIRGINIA. Dr. Fosdick, do you think that if criminals
prayed they would stop being criminals?

DR. FOSDICK. Take yourselves for example. If a boy
gets started on some bad habit and he really wants to
stop, then prayer will help him. But if he does not
care very much and just kneels down and prays, "O God,
help me to be good," it is about like saying, "O God,
give me a million dollars." Prayer does not help unless
you mean it and are ready to do something about it.
When a person really goes down into his inner life and
looks at himself and really wants to change his life,
prayer sometimes helps a great deal.

People have different ways of praying. You don't
have to kneel down to pray; you don't have to be in a
church to pray. A friend of mine said to me one day,
"My way of praying is different from yours." I said,
"How do you pray?" He answered, "Playing the piano
is a prayer to me."

RUTH. Dr. Fosdick, what is God? Of course, I have my own idea, but I would like to know your opinion.

DR. FOSDICK. This God that the scientists talk about I call the far end of God. That is, God way out there. The near end of God, the God that comes close to us and that really matters to us is in our inner life. This is something like electricity. Electricity is way out there in the stars, and it is also here in our room. So God is both far away and very close to us.

One trouble about our thinking of God is that we try to think of Him as having bodily form. I remember one time when my daughter asked me, at the age of five, "Does God have a skin?" "No, of course not," I said. Then my daughter began to laugh very hard, and I could not understand why she was laughing, and I asked her. She said, "Oh, I was just thinking how funny He would look without a skin."

I remember the first time I ever saw God, or thought I saw Him. I was about four. I was standing out on the back stoop, and I saw the stars in the dark sky for the first time. I was sure that I saw both God and Jesus up there in the sky. Each one had a high hat on his head. I ran into the house to tell my mother that I had seen God.

Perhaps it will help us to think about God if we remember that we ourselves are invisible. I am invisible, do you realize that? You cannot see me, the real Harry Fisdick. You cannot see my thoughts, my love, my purposes. I am invisible. You, too, are invisible. No one has ever really seen you. They can't. The most real things in the world are invisible.

Then did you ever realize that you can be in more than one place at one time? I have a daughter in Baltimore. If someone should hurt my daughter there, it would hurt me more than anything you could do to hurt the part of me that is in this room. Part of me is in Baltimore. Part of me is wherever my wife is, or where my friends are.

We are as invisible as God, and we can be in several places at one time.

MICKY. Dr. Fosdick, when do people join the church and why?

DR. FOSDICK. There is no definite time when people join the church. I joined the church when I was seven. Most boys and girls probably do not join the church until they are older, say twelve or fifteen years.

Church is something like a school. We learn better in a school than we do when we are by ourselves because we are all together. It is the togetherness in the church that matters. People are often better Christians when they can come together.

Joining the church is something that you, yourself, must decide about. You already belong to the church in a sense, since you belong to the Church School, but perhaps you have been coming to the Church School because your mothers and fathers thought you ought to come. When you join the church, you do something that you choose to do.

PHYLLIS. Why do we laugh at other people's religion when sometimes our own is just as queer?

DR. FOSDICK. Laughing at other people's religion is a foolish thing to do. Of course, there is much in our own that is not good. There is much in other religions that is very fine. I have a good friend by the name of Rabbi Wise. When I heard him talk about Jesus one night, and tell how much Jesus meant to him, I felt I had much to learn from him. There are a number of Jews that are members of the Riverside Church.

The discussion then turned particularly to conversation about the Jews, and why people were prejudiced against them, and what Dr. Fosdick thought of Hitler and his attitude toward the Jews. By this time the discussion had been going on for over an hour and a quarter and still the children did not seem weary. We served fruit juice and cookies, but that did not interrupt the seriousness of the discussion at all.

### A Panel Discussion:
### "How We Feel Ourselves Inside of Us"

That afternoon's two-hour conversation between the children and their minister was a rare experience for all of us present, including Dr. Fosdick himself. I doubt if it has been forgotten even yet by those who participated in it.

Its worth cannot be measured by the amount the children learned or by the clarity of the convictions they formed. It is rather to be found in the experience we all had shared of standing together "on the shores of wonder" and discovering that we could exchange our intimate thoughts and feelings freely, and discover our minds meeting and our respect for each other deepening. How might we celebrate this unusual occasion? How could the children give further expression to their new insights and wonderings? Could the blessing of our experience be shared in some way with the children who had not been present?

Finally the thought came. Why not let a group of the more capable of the children form a panel to lead a discussion in our next departmental service of worship? The result was some phone calling and a meeting of three of us at the church on Saturday morning to talk over what we might do.

"We could talk a little about ourselves first," suggested Ruth, "then we could ask the rest to give their ideas."

Although we discussed possibilities for about an hour, our ideas were still vague when we separated. I wondered if the other children would feel free to speak up. The three children, at least, were hopeful. So we decided to risk the venture.

### The Service of Worship

At our usual Sunday hour for the departmental gathering we met. On one side of the platform sat the choir, and on the other side around a small table, sat Ruth, Phyllis, Brooks, and I.

First of all we sang a new spring song. "Come Ye Faithful, Raise the Strain."

After this the panel discussion began. The following, although a shortened report, is as nearly verbatim as it was possible to record.

### The Discussion

RUTH. We have been learning here a great deal about cave people and their religion, and about the Hebrews and other people such as the Indians and Egyptians, but we haven't had a chance to talk much about the way *we feel ourselves, inside of us.* Could we talk today about our own ideas of God? Would you tell us how you feel?

(Such an unusual request left the children somewhat stunned. No one seemed able to speak up.)

MRS. FAHS. It isn't always easy to talk about these things we feel inside of us, Ruth, but perhaps we can try.

PHYLLIS. We have our ideas. We know what we think, and then again we are not sure it is true. (*There was still silence. We waited.*)

MRS. FAHS. Perhaps it would be easier if we first told one another of ideas of God *we used to have* when we were younger, and how we feel about these ideas now. (*This seemed to bring release of feelings and thoughts.*)

BROOKS. I used to think of God as being a man up in the sky looking down on the earth, and that he sent Jesus down to the earth to save us. I think now he is more like something inside of us.

PHYLLIS. I did not wonder so much about God as I did about where we go after we die. I was told the story of the Last Supper and I imagined that when we die we would all sit around a table with Jesus. Those who had been good would sit on his right side and those who had been bad would sit on his left. After a while I decided that this was not reasonable. Now I keep on wondering what does happen after we die.

MRS. FAHS. Do you remember, Ruth, when your class was meeting one afternoon with Dr. Fosdick, what he said he used to think God was like when he was small.

BROOKS. I remember what he said about his daughter. One day she asked him, "Father, does God have any skin?" Dr. Fosdick said, "Why no, of course not." Then his daughter began to laugh. He asked her what she was laughing about, and she said, "I was just thinking how funny He would look."

RUTH. When Dr. Fosdick was a little boy he went out at night and looked up at the stars, and he ran back into the house and said, "I have seen God and Jesus." He thought he saw them up in the sky in the clouds. They were both wearing high silk hats.

PHYLLIS. One girl said she used to think God looked like a carrot.

GIRL. [*From group.*] When I was little I used to think God was a great king who sat on a throne up in the sky. He had everything he wanted. Women came around him with baskets of flowers and fruits. He was very kind.

BARBARA. I used to think God was a great big giant, so big he was twice as big as the whole world.

HARRY. Mother told me God was with me, and I could not see how he could spread himself all over.

RUTH. You know you cannot see me. I am invisible. You can only see my face and my body. You cannot see me. Dr. Fosdick told us about a man during the war who had a new idea. He found out how to cure diabetes. Now that idea did a great deal of good and cured many people, but nobody saw that idea. You can't see a thought. You can't see me, either. I can't see you.

MRS. FAHS. Do you mean, Ruth, that we are really something like God? He is invisible and so are we?

RUTH. Yes. And I am in quite a few places at one time. My mother is at home and part of me is there. My grandmother is in the country, and part of me is there.

MRS. FAHS. You mean to say, Ruth, that we can be in more than one place at one time? That we are something like God whom we think of as being everywhere?

RUTH. Yes.

GEORGE. What is prayer?

BROOKS. When I was little, my mother told me to pray every night before I went to bed. I thought praying was a job I had to do. Now when I am alone I pray. I just feel like it.

PHYLLIS. First when I was little mother made a prayer for me. I thought I would have to say just that prayer, or it wouldn't do any good. After that I learned the Lord's Prayer and I always said that. Now I do not think you have to say any one prayer. You do not have to get down on your knees. Prayer is something you can feel anywhere.

RUTH. You do not have to kneel or pray just in the church. Dr. Fosdick says he prays when he is out walking. Our mothers started us by teaching us to pray, but as we grow up we have to work it out for ourselves.

EVELYN. How does praying help?

PHYLLIS. I think if you pray strong enough for a certain thing, praying gives you courage to go out and work up to that thing. You pray for it, and that gives you the courage to get it.

ESTHER. My mother does not believe in God. At night she puts me to bed and opens up the window. When she has gone out of the room, I get out of bed and kneel down and pray. I sneak it in.

MRS. FAHS. Whether or not we shall pray is something each must decide for himself. Since it is something that goes on inside us, nobody can keep us from praying, not even our mothers.

ERDMUTHE. I cannot imagine God and Jesus. I don't see how there can be two such good people.

MRS. FAHS. You mean you do not know which to pray to? That has bothered others too. They have sometimes thought there were two gods, Jesus and God. Sometimes they pray to one and sometimes to the other. Some of us do not think of Jesus as being God. We think he was a man, just like other men, but he was a very good man, the best we have known about. We think that in a way his spirit is living today, but we do not pray to him. Perhaps it will help you if you think of Jesus as a man, and pray to God.

CHILD. [*In group.*] Last summer I went to summer school. The teacher taught us to skip. I said, "I do not think I can do it, not in a century." The teacher said, "Try and God will help you." So I tried, and I did the best in the class. It was just on account of God. I think God helped me a little bit.

GEORGE. It's just like the old proverb, "God helps those who help themselves."

HARRY. There must be someone greater than we are who knows everything. That is God.

RUTH. Someone said if we knew all about God we would be greater than God.

BROOKS. There is one reason. There would have to be someone who controls everything in the universe, and sees that all the things happen that happen.

OSCAR. Did Jesus ever do anything wrong?

MRS. FAHS. How would you go about answering that question for yourself? First, you would study to find out what is reported that Jesus did. Someday you will have this opportunity. Then you would have to decide for yourself, would you not, whether or not you thought what he did was right or wrong?

JOHN. If Jesus did all the miracles the New Testament tells about, why doesn't someone do miracles now?

PHYLLIS. Dr. Fosdick says Jesus was just a great man. What people thought were miracles were just everyday things, but people did not understand them.

There were still a half dozen or more raised hands. Children were wishing for a chance to speak. The interest was intense. Seeing the hands of the clock indicating time to close the service, however, I suggested that those who had questions to ask might write them down and give them to me or to their teachers. We might have this sort of talk together another time if they wished it.

We closed by singing two verses of a hymn which some of the group had asked for, "Our God, Our Help in Ages Past." I said, "This hymn has in it some great thoughts of God."

This service was a high-water mark in spiritual feeling. There was a quiet intensity in the atmosphere that pervaded the assembly.

After the group had begun to move out of the room, two boys came up to me. One said, "I think prayer does good. When I have done something wrong, and I stop to pray, I get courage to admit I have been wrong."

The other said, "I think that praying does good. I know a man who was condemned to die, and he prayed, and it gave him courage to go to the chair."

## The Children's Own Efforts at Prayerful Expression

### We Are Thankful

We are thankful for the sun, and the moon and the stars, but we want more people to look at them and wonder.
We are thankful for plenty of good food to eat,

but we want hungry children to have more.
We are thankful for the flowers and the grass,
but we want more children to enjoy them.
We are thankful for the fun we have,
but we want playgrounds for all children.
We are thankful for the animals,
but we want to take better care of them.
We are thankful for our parents who are so good to us,
but we want all children to be loved.
We are thankful for this great and wonderful world,
but we want more people living in it to be happier. Amen.

Composed by Dorothy Bailey (fifth grade)
(slightly revised)

## The Snow Gets Me Wondering

Sounds came to me from my bed.
I heard tinkling, scraping, shoveling.
I stood up. I looked out of my window.
I was blinded by the great light.
Yesterday the ground was grey.
Today it is white.
Housetops, trees, bushes and hills—
All are covered with a clean white blanket.
To think that God made all this happen
In such a pretty way!
The snow gets me wondering!

Is the snow alive?
It has power to change the world
As no man can ever change it.
Does the snow have feelings?
Does it like to be scraped off the pavement?
Or would it like to lie where it falls?
The snow gets me wondering!

[*NOTE: A very beautiful snow had fallen in the night. I sent a note to each class in the Junior Department asking them to spend a little while first thing in the morning, expressing how they felt about the snow. I asked that someone write down their words and send them to me. I thought perhaps I might put together what they said, and make a poem on "Our Feelings About the Snow" to read in the service of worship. This composite poem was the result.*]

*Up Is Forever*

> Up is forever up, up, up,
> How high is up nobody knows
> The stars and planets are still further up!
> I'd like to know how high is up
> Wouldn't you?
> The constellations are still up, up, up.
> Some people think there is an end,
> But I am sure I don't.
> I like to watch the stars so high up
> Don't you?
>
> Up is forever up, up, up,
> How high is up nobody knows.
> The stars and planets are still further up.
> I'd like to know how high is up.
> Wouldn't you?

> William Ives (ten years old)

*Nobody Knows*

We thought together about beginnings,
And we thought, nobody knows
how anything begins.
How wonderful it is.

We thought about the beginning of life—
the single cell that could grow
and make more cells—
the green scum that was on the water
in the beginning;
about animals growing to be people—
about the cave men—
that they were dirty and hungry and scared;
about all the things that people learned to do,
beginning long ago.
We wondered how we could come from the green scum
that was on the water.
These things are wonderful!

We thought about the baby Jesus,
wrapped in swaddling clothes and lying in a manger,
and we thought about babies,
beginning to live in the world,
growing and being new all the time.
These things are wonderful!

Composed by a group of fourth graders

*We Admire the Animals*

O God, we thank you for the animals, for they seem to us very wonderful.

We admire the monkeys, because they can swing on their tails, and hang on to things with their hands and their feet. They can jump from tree to tree without falling. They use their little hands as we use ours.

We admire the birds because they can fly. They can build their nests close to the ground or high up in the tree tops. They can find worms and seeds to eat, and they teach their little ones all the things they know.

We admire the deer, because they can run very fast. With their good ears they can hear other animals coming through the forest. They make a path to a meeting place where they drink from the water hole.

We admire the kangaroos, because they can leap so far, using their long legs and strong tails. The mother carries her babies in a little pouch, and she knows just how to take care of them.

We admire the beavers, because they can cut down trees with their sharp teeth and make their own homes. They can make dams to protect their houses. They know how to carry mud on their long, broad tails, to make their homes tight and warm.

We admire the camels, because they can live safely in the desert. They can carry water and food to last them a long time. They know what to do when a sandstorm comes up, and then can even protect people in a storm.

We admire all animals, because they can do so many things without the help of man. They can find homes for themselves and take care of themselves. They know where to get water, and how to get the kind of food they like.

O God, we thank you for the animals for they seem very wonderful to us.

> Composed by a class of fifth grade
> children and used in a service of worship.

*These Things Seem Wonderful*

LEADER.  These things seem wonderful!
CHILDREN.  How life can be in tiny specks,
How a bulb can grow into a flower,
How plants and trees can grow.

LEADER.          These things seem wonderful!
CHILDREN.        How caterpillars can grow wings
                    and turn into butterflies,
                 How spiders weave their webs so fine
                    they are hard to see.
LEADER.          These things seem wonderful!
CHILDREN.        How we can go to sleep and waken again,
                 How we can keep things in our minds.
LEADER.          These things seem wonderful!
CHILDREN.        That mothers can have new babies,
                 That twins can be born,
                 That we can see and hear and feel.
LEADER.          These things seem wonderful!
CHILDREN.        How the seasons change!
                 How the universe works!
CHILDREN, LEADER, AND CONGREGATION TOGETHER.
                 "Why, who makes much of a miracle?
                 As for me, I know nothing else but miracles,
                 The fishes that swim, the motion of the waves,
                 To me, every hour of the light and dark is a
                    miracle,
                 What stranger miracles are there?"

                                        Walt Whitman

[*Reported by Ruth P. Koshuk regarding a service at the
Northside Unitarian Church, Pittsburgh, Pa. 1952.*]

*A Children's Psalm*

There is a song in my heart
about the things that make me glad.
I am filled with happiness:
"My cup runneth over."
I must sing a song and thank God.
He gave life to me
as to everything around me.

To those who love me
and to all whom I may love.
Father and mother,
sister and brother, my friends.
Oh my dog, my dog, was there ever one like him?
I like horses, it feels so good to be with them.
The birds—God, how could you dream them all?
Their colors—their song—their flying—
I must sing a song and thank God.
Who kept the first fire? Who first made bread?
Who spoke the first words? Who laughed the first laugh?
Who wept the first tears? Who felt the first wrong?
Who searched for you first, O God?
O, I thank you, God.

[*Note: This psalm grew out of the work of the Fifth
and Sixth Grade Children in the First-Day School of
Montclair, New Jersey.* Friends Intelligencer, *February
2, 1946.*]


## Some Adult Worded Prayers

*The Author's Own Attempts*

God of all, Creator of all,
We would open our minds to what is true
as flowers open their petals to the warm sunlight.
May we learn to think clearly and wisely.
May we learn to feel kindly and considerately.
If a new thought—a true thought—has wakened us today,
may we accept it and live with it as best we can. Amen.

*

We are thankful that there is so much in the world that
we can depend on.

But we are thankful too for the many surprises—for the
things we do not know how to predict.
We are glad for both the sure things and the things we
can not know.
Like the *Yang* and the *Yin* they may both be good.
Together they give us the courage to try and the glow of
adventure.

*

We pause in quiet thoughtfulness
to remember some of the good things that have been given us;
without our asking for them,
without our working for them;
things that we could never make—
things that no person in all the world could make for us—
things meant for everybody to enjoy.
From whence? From whom? How? Why?
There's never an end to our wondering.

*

We are like drops of water in a vast ocean.
God is like the whole ocean.
We are like single leaves on one tree.
God is like all the trees of all the forests
with all their leaves.
We are like single cells in a person's body.
God is like the life in all the cells in the whole body—
even in all the bodies of all persons.
We are all joined together in God.
We are never alone.  We belong together in God.

*

We are thankful for such a man as Jesus.
We are thankful that his birthday is still being remembered.
We are thankful for the good things Jesus stood up for.
We are thankful for his courage, and for his compassion.

We are thankful for the ideas he thought of and talked
about that have started us to thinking and that make us
want to be better persons.

*

We are thankful for the opportunities that have been ours
this day.
May we go to our homes—carrying with us memories
of this wonderful morning together. Amen.


A Few Prayerful Selections
from Ancient Scriptures

*An Egyptian Song of Joy*

Aten was the word for God used by Akhenaten, a
Pharaoh who lived more than 3000 years ago. He
thought of God as the life-giving power seen in the sun.
(Adapted from translation by James Breasted.)

LEADER.    O living Aten, Beginning of Life,
           Thy dawning is beautiful in the horizon of
              heaven.
           Thou art beautiful, great, glittering, high over
              the earth.
           Thou fillest every land with Thy beauty.
           By Thee man liveth.
RESPONSE.   O Thou God of All!
LEADER.    Bright is the earth when Thou sendest forth
              Thy rays.
           The birds flutter in the marshes.
           The fish in the river leap up.
           The sheep dance upon their feet.
           The trees and plants flourish.

RESPONSE.    O Thou God of All!

LEADER.      Though Thou art far off,
               Thy rays are on the earth.
               Though Thou art on high,
               Thy footprints are the day.
               Dawning, shining, far off and returning,
               The world is in Thy hand,
               And Thou art in my heart.

RESPONSE.    O Thou God of All,
               Whose powers no other possesses,
               How excellent are Thy designs,
               O Lord of eternity.
               The world is in Thy hand,
               And Thou art in my heart. Amen.

### God Everywhere

"Whither shall I go from thy Spirit?
Whither shall I flee from thy presence?
If I ascend to heaven, thou art there!
If I make my bed in Sheol, thou art there!
If I take the wings of the morning and dwell in the
uttermost parts of the sea,
Even there thy hand shall lead me,
and thy right hand shall hold me.
If I say, "Let only darkness cover me,
and the light about me be night,"
Even the darkness is not dark to thee,
The night is as bright as the day;
for darkness is as light with thee."

Psalm 139: 7-12

### Sky Music

"The heavens are telling the glory of God;
And the firmament showeth the work of his hands.
. . .

> There is no speech nor language!
> Their voice cannot be heard!
> But their music goes out through all the earth,
> And their words to the end of the world."

Psalm 19: 1-4

## God—The Eternal—All-Knowing

"Before the mountains were brought forth, or ever thou hadst formed the earth and the world, even from everlasting to everlasting, thou art God."

"A thousand years in Thy sight are but as yesterday when it is past, and as a watch in the night."

Psalm 90

## Too Wonderful

> "Three things are too wonderful for me!
> four I do not understand:
> The way of an eagle in the sky,
> the way of a serpent on a rock,
> the way of a ship on the high seas,
> and the way of a man with a maiden."

Proverbs 30:18-19

# CHAPTER SIX

# A Dynamic Global Approach to Religious History

"The whole worshipping world
   is enclosed in the temple of life.
Every living man belongs
   to the congregation of humanity.

. . .

   all equally in good standing
   as native citizens of the universe."
                          Carl J. Nelson[1]

## A Questioning Boy Asks for the Dynamic Way

A group of ten-year-old boys and girls had been discussing the Zuni Indian story of creation. They had
also been discovering how religiously these primitive
people had felt toward the natural world around them.
In the midst of their discussions one morning, Joe, in
a meditative mood, said, "I wonder who was the first
person in all the world to find out about God. I
mean, I wonder who was the very first person ever to
think up the idea of God all by himself."

How often it is that the children are the ones who
spontaneously find the dynamic way of learning while
those of us who are older, with minds already cluttered

with preconceived opinions, have a vision too blurred for any fresh look.

Suppose Joe's question had been asked of a Biblically oriented Sunday School teacher, one whose understanding of man's religious history had been gained primarily through the Judaeo-Christian Bible, what might he have replied? Possibly in some such way as this:

> In the Bible the first man is called Adam. He did not have to think up an idea of God all by himself, however, for Adam actually *saw God* face to face walking in the garden of Eden. Adam watched God create all the animals. God asked Adam to give a name to each one as it was created.
>
> When Adam awoke one day from sleep, he saw God walking toward him, bringing with him the first woman. Both Adam and Eve listened as God told them just what would be right for them to do and what would be wrong. They didn't have to think this out either. God told them plainly. But alas, Adam and Eve disobeyed God, and they were driven out of the garden as a punishment, where they could no longer see God face to face. Since that time God has hidden himself from the people of the earth. Only a very few specially good persons have seen God since that time; yet we all know there is a God because the Bible gives us this story.

A very superficial summing up, indeed, of a traditional interpretation of the opening dramatic chapter in human history as portrayed in the Judaeo-Christian Bible, yet it gives the naked skeletal outline of what has been for centuries the cornerstone on which the full Christian story of salvation rests.

A better informed teacher would have frankly told the story as a myth or allegory, giving the children some understanding of when and why it had been first told. Then the class would have been encouraged to discuss the *ideas* in the story instead of the concrete *facts* related. What was the storyteller trying to say about the first man and woman? If the children failed to understand what was meant, the teacher would probably have tried to explain "the truths" expressed through the story. Having done this, however, as best he could, he would still have failed to answer Joe's question, "Who was the first person in all the world to think up an idea of God all by himself?" According to this Biblical story, Adam and Eve never had to ask.

Joe, however, had assumed that the first person in the world must have been fundamentally the same kind of person as he was. Joe assumed also that since God was invisible now, He must have been invisible to human beings from the beginning. Since he himself was finding it difficult to imagine Divinity, he felt it must have been especially difficult for uncivilized people long ago. How long did it take, he wondered, before some idea of God or of gods dawned upon somebody for the first time? What could have happened to give him a hint?

The entire frame of reference within which Joe's mind was working seems alien to that expressed in the Genesis story. His philosophy and science had given him a strikingly different picture of the universe from that assumed in the Biblical record.

Speaking generally, throughout the Bible, God is assumed. What is right and wrong has also been assumed rather than questioned. Man has been *told*. From the Biblical point of view, man's religious history is not that of one long natural process of experiencing, discovering, and reasoning, or even of intuiting naturally from evidences found, the nature of God. Biblical history is called a story of the "acts of God" and the record of Man's responses to God.

# What Do Historians Now Know about the Beginnings of Religion?

Identifying ourselves with the temper of the modern questioning mind, we ask: Have historians discovered evidences to show that man's religious beliefs actually did grow naturally out of his real emotional and practical needs and hopes, and because of his own very nature, and of the nature of the world into which he was born? If so, what are the earliest evidences that explorers have found? Do these go farther back in time than the period covered by the Judaeo-Christian Bible, namely, before the period when man had already learned how to write down his thoughts on stone or parchment?

A few positive answers to these questions, furnished as a result of recent excavations in Germany, extend the story of man's religious development far back to a time about 100,000 years ago. This surprising statement is based on the fact that archaeologists have found carefully buried human bodies in the doorways to caves, which other evidence shows were inhabited by the Neanderthal cave dwellers, so primitive and presumably apelike that anthropologists long begrudged them the title of *Homo Sapiens*. Furthermore, laid alongside these human bodies have been found gifts of the cave man's patiently wrought flint knives and scrapers, and the bones of bears, carefully arranged as if to form a kind of altar.

Thus it would seem that the awesome experience of dying not only frightened our earliest ancestors 100,000 years ago, it also pricked their dull minds awake enough to stir them to ponder on what it meant to be dead, and some strong urge to live kept them from succumbing to dispair. The dead body was not like the living person. What had happened? Some living inwardness had disappeared. Where was it? Could it be the dead might still be alive, that they could live without their bodies? Had not they, themselves, who still lived often gone out of their bodies when they were asleep? Perhaps dying was like a long, long sleep. It must have been very hard for these dull-minded first people to think about such things. Probably they could not always tell the difference between something they felt or imagined and something they really saw or did. It seems to have helped them to imagine their dead as living on and as visiting them now and then. They wished they could do something for them. So they began putting things down in under the ground with the dead bodies as gifts for them.

Although believing in such invisible ancestral spirits may seem a far cry from a belief in God, yet anthropologists accept this beginning as a first crude step in the natural religious development of man. By acting on this one belief, early man began nurturing his awareness of his own living inwardness. He felt he was spirit as well as body. Thus in spite of much evidence to the contrary, he declared himself immortal. At least he felt there was in him something alive that transcended his mere body.[2] In so doing primitive man added to his own courage and broadened his perspective on life.

Even though belief in a personal immortality need

not be regarded as essential for religious living, nevertheless, some awareness and appreciation of one's inner intangible being, it would seem, are essential. Until one feels the invisible within himself, how can he imagine an invisible spirit of larger dimensions? The mystery of death continues to challenge men.

In caves occupied later by the more intelligent Cro-Magnon cave dwellers, living about 20,000 years ago in what is now southeastern France and northern Spain, even more amazing evidence has been found of man's further courageous experimental venturing with unseen spirits. Historians now give credit to these still primitive hunters for having been the first men known to have definitely set aside a special place for such attempts to communicate with unseen spirits.

The most famous of these places of worship is far back in a large and awesome rocky cavern near the edge of a cliff. There in the deep darkness a few courageous, serious-minded prehistoric men painted and etched on the rock walls their now famous likenesses of their animal contemporaries, using paints and brushes of their own devising, while flickering lights from crude oil lamps or torches of their own making lighted the walls.

One interpretation of these paintings now being given by some leading anthropologists is that these ancient hunters, when standing before the pictures, felt that they were standing before the spirits of the animals they had slain; and by dancing in pantomime before the pictures and by piercing them with their arrows they felt their power to be successful was increased. Also by bringing the animal spirits gifts they were apologizing for having to hunt them. These early men assumed that the animals like themselves had feelings. They expected their revenge, yet man's hunger for animal food was compulsive and the animal furs protected him from the fierce cold.[3] So the gods of these Cro-Magnon cavemen of 20,000 years ago seem to have been the unseen spirits within the animals whom they vaguely felt their hunters' knives had never entirely killed.

## But Why Pass On to Children Such Superstitions?

Whenever a student begins to inquire about any kind of human achievement that has had a long history in different parts of the world, it seems wholly natural sooner or later to inquire how it all began and why. For example, he asks who was the first person who dared to try to fly? Who were the first people to try to write, or to work out an alphabet? Who were the first to measure the movements of the stars and sun and moon?

Understanding the very first steps and the reasons for trying to take them often gives a primary insight into the adventurous and exploratory nature of the entire historical process that is denied one who is exposed primarily, or solely, to those parts of the heritage that have already been characterized as being the best.

At this point it is relevant to note that certain of today's existentialist philosophers, who insist upon a deep and wholly honest realism, have, if I understand their meaning, expressed somewhat similar sentiments. They say: "If you want to understand anything truly, try to examine it as if you were the very first person in all the world to see it." "Empty your eyes" is one of their most arresting ways of expressing the thought. "Empty your eyes of all those second-hand perceptions that others have given you about the thing you want to understand. Then look at it as if you were the very first to see it." Such an effort might be likened to what Emerson described as having "direct relations with the universe."

Such an imaginative venture would be impossible to achieve fully; nevertheless, it is well worthwhile from time to time to strive to accomplish it. The first things are primary. They belong deep in our nature. They contain the seeds of the universals, the likenesses with which we all begin.

## The Dynamic Beginnings of Religion Unknown in Bible Times

The writers of the sixty-six books in our Judaeo-Christian Bible, however, knew nothing of these dynamic, natural beginnings of religion in human experiences. Most of the data now available regarding prehistoric man was not known 100 years ago, and even yet most adults are still unaware of its significance. The Bible, as a whole, covers a relatively brief and partial portion of the history of man's religious development. Beginning shortly before the great Mesopotamian flood (now known to have occurred a little before 3000 B.C.), the Biblical history closes with but a few glimpses beyond 100 A.D. Scarcely 4000 years at most!

Furthermore, although the Bible begins with what is presumed to be the very creation of the whole universe and moves from that to portray the creation of the first animals and the first man and woman, it does not long continue as a universe-oriented story. It is soon narrowed to the story of the Hebrew people, who thought themselves chosen of God to be the world's religious leaders. Later in the New Testament, the Hebrews are rejected as the "Chosen" ones, and their special mission is assigned to believers in Jesus as the "Christ," the one Savior of the world. Furthermore, the brief history given is primarily that of one people, written from the angle of their national and religious biases.

Since the Bible has for centuries been regarded as the main textbook for the religious education of Jews and Christians, the first religious history usually given to Western children begins either with Moses (or with Abraham before him) or Jesus. For both groups the history included is largely confined to the development either of Judaism or of Christianity. In neither case does the history have a universal outreach, except in terms of a future hope of the final conquest of mankind by the beliefs and ideals of one or the other religion.

## Crucial and Far-reaching Changes Are Involved

I still recall vividly my first effort to experiment with a group of nine-year-olds in the Riverside Church School of New York City by introducing them to a truer and broader account of the beginnings of religion in human experience than is given in the Bible alone. I had been doing a good deal of reading of library books depicting the religious customs of primitive peoples, especially about the Bushmen of Africa and the Aborigines of Australia. I had also read everything I could find about the prehistoric cave dwellers of France and Spain. In addition, I took an extension course at the Museum of Natural History under Margaret Mead's leadership.

When the Church School opened in the fall, I began sharing with my new pre-adolescent friends some of the results of my searching. On the basis of the data gathered, I imagined a few concrete vivid stories about these ancient cave dwellers. We all tried to put ourselves imaginatively in the situations they had faced. The children eagerly scanned the illustrations in the library books I brought to class and started painting their own pictures.

I had my difficulties with discipline. It often seemed that there was more playful excitement than understanding. I realized the children were puzzled, wondering why such stories were being given them in Sunday School; but I felt a basic interest on the part of the majority in the class.

Then one morning an unforgettable moment came unexpectedly. One of the keenest and brightest members of the class, a girl who had been a faithful participant in a liberal Christian Sunday School ever since her kindergarten days, the daughter of an important Columbia University professor, exclaimed in the midst of one of our group discussions, *"I never knew before that there was any religion before Jesus."* I confess I was astounded.

The longer I have meditated since on her remark, the more I realize how revolutionary the change was that was beginning to take place in the mind of this child. She did not resist the change. In fact there was the suggestion in her voice that she had experienced an exhilarating discovery. Some weeks later, as the entire class was working out several dramatic scenes to present to the rest of the department in one of our worshipping assemblies, she confided to me her wish that she might help me write a book made up of the stories I had been telling them.

Although I knew that I was not well enough informed to write the kind of book needed, ever since that experience I have been convinced that some sort of books should be written for elementary school children that would interpret for them vividly and dramatically, in the light of the most recent archaeological findings, and anthropological and historical linguistic studies, the fascinating and stirring beginnings of the global story of mankind's changing religious efforts.

## Our Present Educational Situation

For centuries in the Western world, the Judaeo-Christian Bible has been accepted as the major textbook dealing with man's religious past for the religious education of growing children. In other fields of learning, new textbooks are continually being written, and older ones are being radically revised. Biased interpretations of historical events have been corrected and more scholarly and objective points of view have been injected into the historical records in the light of the most recent findings from historical research.

In the area of religion, however, our Bible has been regarded as too sacred to revise; or it is revered so sentimentally that there is strong resistance even to trying to discover the unbiased facts of the history that the records have so often distorted. It is the "literature" and the myths of the Bible rather than man's true history that seem still to be most wanted. The recent findings of archaeology and anthropology and historical linguistic criticism have scarcely begun to be taken seriously or dynamically.

Furthermore, in secular subjects, children have been led to respect first steps, and the first men who had the initiative, courage, and insight to risk taking them. When studying religion, however, children have often been led to feel that the crude beginnings in religion were superstitious, idolatrous, and unworthy even of attention. Adults have been so concerned to give children what they themselves had already been assured was the best religion that the tendency has been to omit the beginning sections, the cruder religious practices and beliefs, and to dwell exclusively on what has supposedly been accepted as the true religion. Thus religious history for many has become a carefully chosen collection of "the best" heirlooms, as it were, preserved in the world's libraries and museums. To be intelligent about these heirlooms of *our own religious sect* and to reverence them has become almost a kind of insignia by which to distinguish the religious person from the irreligious one.

Thus far in the *Beacon Series in Religious Education* this more universal dynamic outlook has been but partially implemented, yet a natural and universal philosophy regarding the development of religion is thoroughly imbedded in the books written for use during the early years of childhood.

In our liberal Schools of Religion before the children begin any historical study they are encouraged and guided into the dynamic process of feeling their own way into a philosophy of life; and later toward thoughts of Divinity by having some of their own most significant and thought-provoking experiences accented through discussions of dramatic stories of imaginary children, both male and female, who symbolize real children anywhere. Although the word *God* is seldom mentioned during these early years, the books for preschool children and for those aged six, seven, and eight stimulate alert, exploratory attitudes, and encourage the children's meditation and analysis of real and natural experiences with the natural world of things and people. We, therefore, hope that children who relive these stories imaginatively will themselves be awakened to experience dynamically the beginning of religious feelings in their own daily living.

When the time comes later for them to study the experiences of persons of the past who were also religious, we hope they will sense some affinity with them. Instead of leading each oncoming generation to learn primarily about its own particular religious Scriptures in order that they may become better Christians, Jews, or Buddhists, etc., we believe each generation should be exposed to a wider, more dynamic, and truer story of the past so that they may better understand the processes by which changes were brought about, both those of creative renewal and those leading to stagnation and degeneration. To accomplish this understanding we believe the story should become global in its outreach rather than limited to a particular preferred religion.

Such basic and large revisions, however, call for the best minds and the most deeply perceptive students of history who can be found, or who can be developed. It is a truly serious, complex, and demanding proposal. But the time has come. Mankind is rapidly becoming globally minded in other fields of interest. Religious conflicts are still among the most sinister threats to man's survival. The age-old practice of developing exclusive religious loyalties, based primarily upon cultural or national inheritances and on emotional attachments, is dangerously inadequate. Even in this twentieth century in all religious groups, the majority of adherents are still ignorantly prejudiced against religions other than their own. Just as fanatic forms of nationalism must go, so must fanatic forms of religious loyalty be dispelled.

However, for any group to introduce this more universal element into the education of both children and adults involves an amount of intelligent creative labor, devotion and research, the writing of new books, guided experimentation in new ways of teaching, and leadership training that are beyond the present imagination of our best educators and religious leaders.

## Some First Steps Toward Making Our Dreams Come True

While the great tasks of research and experimentation are being initiated, what can we do who are serving now in relatively obscure ways in local churches and

synagogues? Can we prepare the way for the longer
and harder climb?

The leading of a gathering of children for worship
may seem of small significance. The telling of one
newly-found story of mankind's early religious experiences (such as those following this chapter) may seem
of small account, yet let us begin. New teachers are
continually being enlisted to teach in our Schools of
Religion who have not yet fully assimilated into their
own living the meaning of this exploratory natural way
of developing one's religion. Their use of the books in
the *Beacon Series* may be rather perfunctory. Through
hearing a few imaginary historical stories of man's
earliest efforts in the life of the spirit not only may
some children be awakened by an unforgettable experience, but some inexperienced class teacher's understanding of this more dynamic philosophy for studying
man's religious past may be engendered, a new fervor
aroused, and new insights may be gained to enliven his
future teaching for weeks to come.

We may also hope that some of the children themselves will have the know-how and the deep spiritual
insight required for dynamic leadership in the years
ahead.

## Illustrations from Experience: Four Imagined Stories of the Beginnings of Religion in Human Experience

During the last century over one hundred caves
have been discovered in Europe alone, whose rocky
walls are still covered by etchings and paintings made

by our primitive ancestors some fifteen to twenty thousand years ago. Some are still so remarkably well preserved and were executed by these primitive artists with such amazing skill and artistic feeling that they speak to us with a vividness that words could scarcely excel.

The stories I venture to present in the following pages are imagined accounts of what some of these etchings and paintings seem to tell. The actual people named in the stories never really lived, of course; yet possibly others somewhat like them did live; men and women and children who had had experiences essentially like the ones portrayed, and who thought and felt about such experiences in much the same ways as the story characters think and feel.

Anyone retelling the stories should, for his own sake, do reading of his own in some of the many good books now in libraries and museums describing and illustrating how archaeologists today interpret these cave paintings and etchings. My amateur stories are offered primarily as suggestions, a starting point from which others may do their own imaginings.

If the children have already studied about these early Cro-Magnon ancestors in their weekday schools, they will be pleased to recount some of their knowledge. The purpose in imagining these particular stories is to portray what we may call the "religious beginnings" in primitive experiences, a phase of the life of our early ancestors not likely to be well presented in our public schools. I am assuming that some curiosity about how these early people began to be religious will have been already aroused before any such narratives are told.

The four stories have been based upon four major kinds of experiences: first, man's first puzzlement and wonderings about a vague something within himself (and apparently in every other living thing) that is intangible and invisible. His experiences in dreaming apparently were significant as challenges to such wondering. Second, this feeling of his own inwardness apparently led early man to feel that animals also had feelings, but this sense of kinship with the animals conflicted with man's need to kill them for food and his own protection from the cold. He tried, therefore, to communicate and keep on friendly terms with them. Third, another type of experience came with sickness, pain, and the need to experiment to find ways of healing; and finally there were man's experiences with the ultimate mystery of death, involving again experimentation and the development of belief in life beyond the physical. These are four basic types of universal human experience out of which religious feelings grew just as naturally as plants grow from seeds.

Other types of experience might have been portrayed in the stories that follow. These were chosen because they are so clearly suggested by the paintings and etchings in the ancient caves. If such stories are told in services of worship or to individual classes, I suggest that the leader find at least one printed sample of a cave drawing to illustrate each story. If possible it should be thrown upon a screen by means of an opaque projector in order to focus attention throughout the telling. The pictures that suggested the stories are among those found in the Lascaux Caves and those in the Caves of the Three Brothers (Les Trois Frères) near Montesquieu-Avantès, France.

### They Dance a Reindeer Dance

Far up near the top of a hill Kungu was sitting under the shelter of an overhanging rock. With a sharp piece of flint he was etching a reindeer on a piece of tusk.

His younger brother Gar was chipping into shape a hard chunk of flint to use as a spear head. His sister, Urg, was sewing two pieces of bearskin together with a bone needle her mother had shaped. Her thread was made of wild pig's tendons. Several youngsters were toddling about, throwing sticks and stones into a fire. Every little while they would bump into each other or stumble on the rough ground and squeal.

The day was chilly. All were glad for a blazing fire, and the three workers kept their blankets of bearskins well wrapped about their knees.

The women of the tribe and the other older children were off hunting firewood and roots. The men were on the chase of bison. Kungu and Gar had been left in charge. The air was clear, washed pure by the morning's rain. As the three worked, each at his own handicraft, they sang a monotonous song.

Breaking his silence, Kungu said: "Gar, tomorrow Chief Mong says I can go into the big cave with him and the other men."

"What, has the time come? Must you be a man tomorrow?" asked Gar in surprise.

"Yes, just that," said Kungu. "Mong said to me this morning, 'Your time has come. Tomorrow you must enter the place of mystery.' "

"Oh, Kungu," cried Gar, clutching his brother's

arm. "Aren't you scared? What if you never come out again?"

"My dream, the one I have been longing for, came to me last night, Gar. I am no longer afraid."

"Your dream, Kungu, tell me!"

"After I had dreamed I felt as though I could have climbed down the cliff alone. I could have run faster than any deer. I could have shot my arrow straight into the heart of any animal I saw."

"Kungu, how could you feel so strong?"

"Last night, Gar, I saw him! He touched me!"

"What did he look like, Kungu?"

"He was beautiful and strong, like a great reindeer with the longest antlers I have ever seen. I saw him leaping across the marsh straight at me. When he came, he stopped and spoke to me as a person speaks. He asked me to run with him to the spring."

"Could you keep up with him, Kungu?"

"Yes. Strange to say, my feet seemed to be wings. Then at the stream we drank together, the reindeer and I. He rubbed his horns against my side in a friendly way. 'I am your friend,' he said. 'I have power over all the reindeer who roam into this valley.'

"Then suddenly the reindeer faded out of my sight. I was left standing alone beside the bubbling spring. I could still see his antlers in the water. I knew, Gar, that I had seen one of the Unseen Ones, and I felt strong."

Kungu looked straight at his young brother, but his eyes did not really see. Gar shrank back half afraid. He seemed to see his older brother grow into a man before his very eyes.

Kungu was dreaming his dream over again. He began again to etch away on the little reindeer tusk.

As the sun was slowly falling down to meet the hills in the west, the hunting party was scrambling wearily up the cliff.

They flung themselves and their weapons down before the open fire. A little wild horse was all they had brought back with them, a scant meal for a couple of dozen hungry mouths.

Two of the men had scarcely more than skinned the carcass and begun chopping it into chunks when squabbling began. They pushed and scolded and filled the air with loud, cross words. They fought for pieces to hold on sticks over the fire. Before the meat was half cooked they began grabbing for chunks to gnaw, each man fearing he would get none at all.

Finally the old chief called aloud above the noise. All became still. Chief Mong had a strange power over his people.

"Brothers, we should not snarl at one another. Let us face our plight as brave men should. Prepare yourselves. We must dance the reindeer dance. Then the Unseen Ones will come near us. They will give us their strength. When we lie down to sleep we shall see them and they will talk to us."

"Good words," they shouted. "We will do whatever you say, Chief Mong. You can do anything." They had not forgotten how often he had made them feel strong. They could always do great things after they danced.

Kungu watched his chief's face as he spoke. "How could a man be so strong?" he thought. "I will stay close beside him. I will do whatever he says."

So the reindeer dance began. Men pulled deer-skins from dark corners in their cave shelter and flung them over their bodies. They daubed each other's faces with white paint, and they marked red designs upon their breasts and backs. The women and the children sat apart near the entrance. They clapped their hands together or drummed big stones with heavy bones as the men danced and leaped in a circle about the fire. Two among the men masked their faces in deer heads. The big graceful horns waved grandly in the air as they danced.

From time to time the men changed the form of their dancing. Sometimes only the two masked men danced, playing with each other's antlers as deer play. Sometimes part of the group were hunters and pretended to throw spears and arrows at the deer. Sometimes all the men pranced as deer around the fire.

Kungu sat with Gar and the other children. He explained to them what the men were doing, and how the Unseen Ones would come. The youngsters were comforted and stopped their crying. Kungu thought to himself, "Next time I shall be one of the dancers. Gar will have to keep the children then."

The monotonous drumming and the dancing lasted hour after hour. The longer they danced the happier and the stronger the hunters felt. Finally, late in the night Chief Mong lifted his hand and called, "It is enough. Take your rest, sleep and dream."

So the dancing ended. Soon all was still under the shadow of the great rock. One lonely watcher kept the fire burning. The others slept and dreamed.


*Kungu Etches His Prayer on the Cave Wall*

When morning came and the sleepers had wakened, Chief Mong called them together, "Light your torches. Gather your paints and brushes and etching flints. Follow me into the cave."

Holding up Kungu's reindeer tusk he said, "This is Kungu's dream picture! See how clearly his eyes have seen and how well his fingers have worked. Today he shall paint *his* picture on the cave walls."

A great shout went up from the crowd of eager men. Chief Mong held high his burning torch, and led the way boldly down into the darkness. Tingling with wonder in every inch of his body, Kungu followed close behind.

One by one the men slowly dropped down into the dark hole. The passageway was steep and narrow. They had to feel their way cautiously. Kungu could touch the cold damp walls on either side as he edged his way along behind the chief. Down, down, down the rocky steps they went into the black dark. Was this the world where the Unseen Ones lived? He dared not ask. None among the men spoke a word. He could hear no sound but the shuffling of feet upon the damp earth and the soft dripping of water off somewhere at a great distance.

Finally, to Kungu's great wonder, Chief Mong led the way into a large high cavern. He could not see the end. Overhead hung hundreds of limestone pendants that glistened in the flickering light like great icicles. From the floor arose white stone pillars as if to meet the beautiful pendants hanging from above.

Never before had Kungu seen so beautiful a place. What wonders these Unseen Ones could perform to shape out of hard stone such beautiful pendants and pillars as these! Kungu was ready to believe anything. He was surely in the secret dwelling place of wonder.

After a moment of silence, Chief Mong took

Kungu by the hand and led him in and out among these ghostly pillars and around the outer wall of the great hall. By the light of the torch which he held in one hand, he showed Kungu the outlines of drawings etched or painted upon the walls. There were pictures of bison and bears, many of them. There were mammoths and horses, tigers and elks. Even owls' heads and many, many reindeer. It seemed as though the pictures were everywhere, on the ceiling, on the walls, on the pillars, and on the floor.

"Each man has drawn the Unseen One who appeared to him in his dream," said Chief Mong. "You must do the same, Kungu. As you etch his picture, he will make you feel strong."

Then the chief searched for a part of the wall where no one else had made a drawing. He commanded two of the men to stand by Kungu while he painted his picture and to hold their torches so that he could see to do his work.

Kungu took out from his bag the little piece of bone on which he had etched his drawing of his dream reindeer. This was his copy. He would make a larger reindeer on the cave wall just like this little one.

He took a piece of flint between his fingers and timidly began his work. At first he made faint marks to show where he would etch the head or the antlers or the legs. Then, when he had made the main outline, he began to etch deeply. Slowly there appeared on the wall before him the form of a graceful reindeer with its head and neck bending down toward the ground.

"The deer is drinking from the spring," thought Kungu. "In my dream the Unseen One and I drank together." As the figure of the reindeer of his dream grew clearer, Kungu felt as though it were really right there once more. He felt as if the horns really touched his body again. He felt strong as Chief Mong had said.

Other men began etching pictures, too, of the Unseen Ones of their dreams. Some etched figures on the floor of the cave. Some worked in awkward positions under low roofs making pictures on the ceilings.

Kungu did not notice when Chief Mong disappeared. He had thought of nothing but his reindeer until someone called, "Where has Chief Mong gone?" Not finding him, they became alarmed. Who would lead them back to the light? Strange as it might seem, however, Kungu was not afraid.

By this time most of the men had finished their drawings and were wandering about. Kungu was touching up his picture a bit here and there. He felt pleased. His reindeer seemed alive.

Suddenly at the end of the great cavern, there flashed a light. Chief Mong reappeared from behind a high ledge. Presently he was standing among them. "Follow me," he called. Raising his torch, he led the men around the walls of the cave.

"Thank them now one by one for their flesh. They have given us their lives. Touch them all, all the pictures, as you pass by them, so that their strength may enter into you. As you touch them, remember the Unseen Ones are yours."

So the procession began slowly making its way around the great cavern. As the men moved past the pictures, they reached out their hands and touched them. All the while they chanted a low monotonous song of thanks.

When the hall had been encircled, the men filed slowly into the narrow, dark, low passageway through which they had come down. Up and up and up they stumbled and climbed, creeping over the rough stones. As they neared the top a speck of grey softness at the end of the long low tunnel gradually became larger and larger.

At last the men climbed out into the light of the world they had left. Their women and children were standing by, watching and waiting anxiously for their return. Gar and Urg jumped with delight when once more they saw Kungu safe and sound. But there was a strange look in his eyes. They stepped back half afraid. He did not seem to see them. He walked away alone into the woods.

### Chief Mong Tries to Be a Doctor

Introduction

When in our actual experience this story was first told, we threw on the screen by means of an opaque projector a copy of the picture of what is usually called "The Sorcerer" taken from the book, *The Art and Religion of Fossil Man,* by Luquot.

I referred to the fact that we had been thinking a good deal about doctors, and I thought that perhaps the children would be interested to see a picture of what many people think is perhaps the first doctor in all the world. It is a picture which explorers have found on the wall of a cave in France. They think it was painted by some cave men perhaps twenty thousand years ago.

When the picture was shown, it evoked a hearty laugh from the children. This was most natural since the figure is half man and half animal. I pointed out to the group that he had the ears of a fox, the tail of a wild horse, the horns of a reindeer, and his hands were hidden within the paws of a bear.

I asked the children if they had ever tried to make up a story about a picture. I said that this was what I had tried to do about this one; that I had read a number of books by men who had studied about the cave people of long ago; and I had tried to put into the story some of the things that the writers think must have been true about the cave dwellers.

## The Imagined Story

The first big hunt of the season had ended with great success. The strong men of the tribe had climbed back up to their cave homes high on the rocky ledge of the hillside shouting wildly in their excitement and bragging of their hunting skill. They had been impatient to reach their camp, to skin the slain animals, and to fill their hungry bodies with food after the long winter when they had had so little to eat.

The feasting was boisterous beyond words. The men quarrelled over the biggest pieces and ate until their bodies bulged with all that they could hold. When at last they were all so full that they could scarcely walk about, they sprawled on the grass and went to sleep. The next morning long after the sun had risen high above the hill beyond the river, the hunters slept lazily on.

There was work, however, for the stay-at-homes to do. The women were scraping with their flint scrapers the skins of the animals the men had slain. When the skins were cleaned at last, the women spread them out on the ground to dry in the sun. Meanwhile, the children ran about from one group of women to another curiously asking questions and now and again stroking rather timidly the long bear fur or lifting the antlers of a deer. One lone old man worked away with the women. His body was too stiff that day to let him go on the hunt with the young hunters.

As the women and Chief Mong scraped away on the skins, they swayed their bodies to and fro, humming monotonously. While they were working, a woman ran up to the old man and spoke to him.

"Father," she said, "the swiftest of our runners does not sleep as the other hunters; he is moaning. He says that there is a burning inside him and a great hurt in his head."

Then a dark frown covered the old man's face. Dropping his knife, he lifted himself with the help of a strong stick and stood before the sleeping hunters. "Wake up!" he cried. "Brothers, we have done wrong. Last night in our hunger we forgot how the animals feel about us and our killing them. We did not stop to ask their pardon for killing them. Instead we shouted loudly over our success. We bragged of our great powers. The unseen spirits of the animals we have slain are angry with us. We must pray to be pardoned. Wait here for me. Let none of you touch the skins or any of the pieces of bone or flesh that are still lying here until I return."

Then the old-man-whose-heart-was-strong picked up a stick from the ground, and walking over to the fire that was still burning in front of the opening to the big cave, he held the stick over the fire until it began to burn.

He then walked over to where the sick young

hunter was lying and moaning. He leaned over and looked into the flushed and dreamy face of the young man—the swiftest of all their runners—as he lay wrapped in a skin.

"Rest unafraid, my son," the old man said as he touched the hot forehead. "We will make amends to the animals for our wrongdoing. Then they will stop punishing you. Once more you will skip over the hills —the swiftest of all our runners."

As the people of the clan watched and listened, they knew that another day for praying to the offended animals had come. The old-man-whose-heart-was-strong chose two young fellows to accompany him into the cave. The rest watched them and their burning torches disappear into the dark earth.

Obedient to the old man's command, no one spoke. The time of waiting seemed long, but they were too awed and anxious to sleep again, and too full of questions they dared not ask to close their eyes.

At last three figures walked out of the darkness. Could the leader be their old father? Could he even be a man? Yes, there was the long shaggy beard, but his ears were the ears of a fox. And he had the tail of a wild horse. On his head were the branching horns of a reindeer, and on his body was skin like a deer's, and his hands were covered by the heavy paws of a bear.

Without a word, the old man walked over to the open space where the pieces of fur, which the women had been scraping, were lying about. Holding out his bearish paws toward these pieces of fur, as if they were alive, he began walking round and round them.

Then he paused and called, "Foxes, foxes, listen to me. You and I wear the same covering on our heads. We eat alike. We sleep alike. You, too, must kill in order to eat. Pardon us that we must kill you to live. Pardon us for our greediness and our bragging in our great hunger. Come back, foxes, come back and be born again in other foxes. We pray you forget our killing."

Again the old-man-whose-heart-was-strong danced around the pieces of skin on the ground. Again he paused and called, "Bear, bear, listen to me. You and I wear the same covering on our hands. We eat alike. Forgive us for our greediness and bragging in our great hunger. Come back, come back and be born again in other bears. We pray you forget our killing."

Again the old-man-whose-heart-was-strong danced round and round the pieces of skin. A third time he paused and called. "Reindeer, reindeer, listen to me. You and I wear the same skin and horns. We eat alike. We sleep alike. You too must kill in order to live. Pardon us that we must kill you. Pardon us our greediness and our bragging in our great hunger. Come back, come back, O reindeer, and be born again in other reindeer. We pray you to forget our killing."

Then the old man fell to the ground exhausted. His lips moved as he lay for a while on the ground, as if he were whispering to the spirits of the animals that he believed were around him.

After a while he rose and walked back to the entrance to the cave, where, wrapped in a blanket of skins, the young man, the swiftest of all the runners, was lying wide awake and feverish. The old man touched him and said, "Young man, the angry spirits are gone. They have pardoned our greediness. They have forgotten our bragging. You will now grow strong again. The burning inside you will die away. Once more you will be the swiftest of our runners."

The young man looked up with wonder in his eyes. He was no longer afraid. He felt a little better.

Then the old-man-whose-heart-was-strong and his two companions went again into the darkness beyond the opening of the cave. When a short while afterwards they came forth into the light, they looked like themselves and they acted like themselves. It was not until the next day, however, that the young man felt strong enough to walk about the camp. By the third day, he was running again with the antelopes.

So perhaps in the days of long, long ago—20,000 years ago—when our ancestors lived in caves, the first doctor might have been a little like this old-man-whose-heart-was-strong, and who helped those who were more timid to keep their hearts strong too.

### Notes on the Story

This strange painting of the first doctor known to man was discovered high on the walls of a spacious cavern in the Pyrenees, called Les Trois Frères because the cavern was first discovered accidentally by three brothers. See *On the Track of Prehistoric Man* by Hubert Kuhn (Random House, 1955) for more details.

Who could have painted it? This is the unanswerable question. Perhaps it was the man himself who became the first healer and priest, as suggested in this story. Perhaps it was one of his followers, some especially gifted and persistent artist, who had often gone with the old man into the cavern to ask forgiveness of the animal spirits and who painted it after the old man's death so that whenever those who lived after him went into this very dark inner chamber of the cave, they would see this painting and feel that their old doctor was still with them.

Now that thousands of years have passed since that time, our doctors have learned many truer things about sickness and what causes it; yet how much more they have yet to learn. A doctor still needs to be a person whose heart is strong, for we find that when we are sick it helps if someone comes to encourage us and to help us not to be afraid.

## Will Kungu Come Back?

### An Explanatory Comment

As indicated in the preceding chapter, evidences have been found to show that the practice of burying gifts alongside the remains of the dead developed among the Neanderthals (in what is now called Germany) thousands of years before the period represented by the art work on the walls of the caves in the French Pyrenees. By 20,000 B.C. such burials may have become routine among the Cro-Magnons; we do not know. For the sake of simplicity, I have taken the liberty of disregarding the dates, since the primary purpose in imagining such stories has been to awaken imaginative feeling for first experiences with some of the primary mysteries of life, among which man's experiences with death have been the most profound. It seemed fitting to make this experience of death the climax of the series.

### The Story

It was late in the summer. None of the men had gone hunting for a long time. The small bits of animal food left from the last hunt were all spoiled, and had been buried out of sight. Everyone was tired of roots and dried berries and fruits. Not having enough to eat made them cross and quarrelsome.

"We must bring back a wild boar or a reindeer today," said old Chief Mong. Everyone was eager to be off. Especially young Kungu, Chief Mong's favorite grandson, who had been allowed but once before to accompany the men on their hunting expedition.

With shoutings and gusto, the hunters started down the path leading to the valley, each man carrying in one hand a big killing stone, and in the other a long spear which he had made.

Left behind on the ledge were the women and the younger children. The women soon scattered along the paths leading farther up the mountain to gather sticks and roots. The children followed along or played a sort of tag together, all except Gar and Urg, two of the older young people who were not quite old enough to go on the hunt.

Gar picked up a piece of a reindeer's antler which he had already scraped smooth and began etching upon it with a sharp flint stone the figure of a reindeer. Urg began scraping a small bone with a flint scraper, trying to sharpen it at one end for a needle. As they worked away, they began to talk together.

"Chief Mong should have let me go on the hunt

today. I'm big and strong enough, and I've already killed a reindeer myself."

"What's that you're saying, Gar?" said Urg. "You know very well you've never shot a reindeer."

"But I *did* shoot a reindeer. It was just the other night. I went alone up the mountainside with my spear. I found a reindeer in the path. I threw my spear and pierced his neck."

"If you did, Gar, we never saw the reindeer. You never brought it back to the cave."

Gar was puzzled. What had happened to that reindeer, he wondered.

"You must have shot it while you were asleep, Gar. Killing a reindeer when you are asleep is much easier than killing one when you are awake."

"But I wasn't asleep, Urg. Didn't you see me get up in the night and go off into the woods?"

"No! And what's more you never did go off that way in the night. You were sleeping in the cave along-side of me all the night through."

It was very puzzling.

"There is something very strange about me, Urg. I can lie quietly in the cave, and at the same time I can go wandering off into the woods."

As Gar tried to think, a strange feeling came over him. He felt as if he had seen something wonderful just for a moment, and then it was gone. It was very hard for a cave boy to think.

Then Gar began etching the picture again on the reindeer's antlers. The two worked away for quite a while without either saying a word.

Presently they heard rustling of branches down below in the valley. Soon there was added the sound of voices. They rose and looked over the cliff. To their surprise they saw the hunters returning. Then they heard moaning and weeping added to the talking. What could the matter be?

Presently they could see the tall form of Chief Mong. On his shoulders he was carrying something. What was it? A wild boar? Gar and Urg waited in suspense.

Finally the old Chief stepped up on to the ledge. Then Gar and Urg saw what it was on his shoulders. The limp body of Kungu! Chief Mong laid it down gently on the ground. Gar and Urg leaned over him. "Kungu! Kungu!" they cried. "Speak! What is the matter?" But Kungu did not hear. His eyes were closed. He did not move. "A reindeer ran after him," explained the chief. "It caught him! Hurled him in the air! Kungu is dead." Great big tears fell on the old man's heavy beard. "And it was only his second hunt! Poor Kungu!"

Soon a crowd had gathered about the lifeless form. Some stood staring and speechless. Others ran screaming up the hillside. One of the hunters began scolding the old chief. "You should have listened to us. You should not have carried Kungu's body all this way up the cliff. The way we have always done is better. You should have left the body where the reindeer left it. Kungu is dead. What we see lying on the ground there is no good. Kungu is gone."

"It is time for us to do differently," said the old chief, "Kungu is not gone. He will come back to us if we are good to him. Let us keep his body close beside us in the cave."

At this some of the men would have taken Kungu's body and thrown it over the cliff, but Chief Mong was too strong for them.

"Go into the cave," he said to two of the men, "and dig a hole near the doorway." "Bring a cup of red paint," he said to another. "We will paint his body from head to foot. Kungu loved red paint."

The young men were accustomed to obeying the orders of the chief, but he had never before given such strange commands.

"Bring one of the big reindeer skins, lying in the cave! We will wrap Kungu as he has been accustomed to be wrapped."

"Foolishness!" cried one of the more daring men. "We need all the warm skins we have for ourselves. They will do Kungu no good."

"But Kungu needs warmth, too," said the old chief with firmness. "Kungu will come back, if we are good to him. He will help us in our hunting.

"Bring his hatchet and his spear, too, and the chain of shells which he made with his own hands! We will put them with him into the ground."

"What a waste," said another in disgust. "Think of the hours and hours he has spent making his spear and his hatchet, and his shells! We need these things ourselves. He can never use them again."

"You are wrong!" shouted the chief. "Kungu needs these things, too. He is not gone. He will come back to us if we are good to him and he will help us in our hunting."

Then Chief Mong and Gar and Urg painted Kungu's body a beautiful red, and when the paint was dry they wrapped him in the big reindeer skin.

They lifted the body and carried it into the cave and laid it in the hole they had dug. Alongside they laid his hatchet and his spear. They put the string of shells around his neck. Then, as they looked for the last time on Kungu's quiet, unanswering face, Chief Mong repeated the words, "Kungu *will* come back. We have been good to him."

Strange to say, that very night, Gar had another dream. Again he arose in the night and wandered off alone in the woods with his spear. As he moved along quietly watching sharply for some wild beast, he saw to his surprise, Kungu walking toward him.

"I have come back to help you hunt," said Kungu. As Gar walked along it seemed to him that Kungu was walking beside him. Gar felt strong and unafraid. Presently he spied, down beside a brook, a reindeer drinking. He ran stealthily toward the deer. He drew his spear. It entered the reindeer's heart.

At this Gar was so excited that he awoke. For a moment he was puzzled. But he was sure he had really seen Kungu! Kungu *had* come back. Kungu had helped him hunt!

Gar could scarcely wait until the old chief had wakened. He ran to him and cried, "Kungu did come back. I saw him last night. He helped me shoot a reindeer."

Then the old chief smiled. "I knew Kungu would come back if we were good to him. Today, Gar, you may go with us on the hunt."

Soon again the hunters set forth down the cliff and along the river. This time they were successful and brought home a good-sized reindeer. The tribe had enough and more than they could eat for several days.

Then one day Gar and Chief Mong were seen walking together into the cave. Gar was carrying a stone cup in which was burning fat that shone like a candle. Chief Mong was carrying another stone cup, filled with red paint made from ground stone and water, and a small flint etching stone.

Near the place where they had buried Kungu's body, they found an unused part of the rocky wall. There the old chief began etching the outline of a bear.

This picture, Gar felt, was like a thank you to Kungu. It was also like a prayer to him asking him to come back again and to help them when they went hunting. In those days men could not write their prayers in words. But they could make them into pictures, pictures made 20,000 years ago.

# CHAPTER SEVEN

# Worshipful Celebrations and Climaxes

As the idea of worshipping has been expanded in the preceding chapters it has included a variety of deepening experiences embracing self-examination, struggle, doubting, trusting, questioning, desiring, purposing, and reverencing. We shall now consider worshipping primarily as thanksgiving and celebration. Individually and in groups we need, now and again, exhilarating moments for remembrance and the celebration of beauty and greatness. We need also occasional climaxes in life's experiences when our hearts expand with the glow of personal fulfillment. This final chapter then is devoted to an examination of several types of worshipful celebrations and climaxes that seem appropriate, needed, and satisfying in a year's calendar of events in a School of Religion.

## Historical Celebrations

Each religious society or sect develops its own holy days for the celebration of the great moments in its history. For many children in the Western world, the ceremonies woven around these annual events have become the most outstanding expressions of the meaning of religion. Christmas and Easter, Hanukkah and Passover, have been for us the most emphasized.

As long as the historical events commemorated continue to be a true source of inspiration to those who remember them, these annual celebrations can have rich meaning. With the changing religious atmosphere of our times and with revised interpretations of these historical events becoming necessary, however, their celebration has become for some of us a serious and unresolved problem. For example, the Christmas legends having been stripped of their former depth of meaning with our more scientific outlook upon the nature of life, we tend increasingly to be satisfied at Christmastime with the mere outward pageantry of the Christmas stories and with the season's accustomed forms of gaiety, while we forget the real historical nature of the event we are celebrating.

When I first actively joined the Unitarian Association it was surprising to me to discover that the problem of rethinking the legendary stories upon which the celebration of Christmas has traditionally rested presented more difficult emotional problems for many than seemed to be involved in rethinking ideas of God. I had expected to find among religious liberals a greater readiness and even eagerness to be realistic in celebrating the birth of the human Jesus than I had found among adherents of other Protestant denominations. I had expected that Unitarians would wish to celebrate the birthday of Jesus in a manner somewhat analogous to the way in which they celebrated the birthdays of other great men. Instead of their continuing to rehearse with children the unbelievable legends regarding a supernatural birth, I had anticipated a desire to celebrate the greatness of his personality as an adult by dramatizing in some impressive way the impact of his teachings upon the history of mankind.

I found, however, that strong emotions were still entwined around the dramatic stories of this one exceptional babe, and around the mysterious peculiar miracle of his unique birth. This was not because Unitarians believed these miraculous legends as historical, but because they were still emotionally attached to them, perhaps as symbols of the mysterious wonder of the birth of all babies and children. Outwardly, superficially, the day was still linked with the birth of the world's miraculous Savior, but inwardly it had become a special day for expressing a general sentimental happiness in all children. Christmas had become our annual Children's Day.

Although this discovery on my part was a disappointment at the time, it led to a greater hope of finding a way by which religious liberals might develop more appropriate ways of celebrating the birth of the human Jesus. Instead of emphasizing the unreality of the unique miraculous birth of one child, why not, in religious circles at least, accent the thought that Christmas should be a day of remembrance of the *Miracle of the Birth of Every Human Child?* Christmas is the day when we give presents to everyone in the family, and when we send remembrances to many others as well. Ideally we hope everyone will receive at least one gift from someone who is happy he was born. Without realizing what we had been doing, we had actually made Christmas everybody's birthday!

The Christmas dramatic program reported on the pages following this chapter was based upon such a revised conception of Christmas. Indeed it seems more in harmony with the oft repeated conviction regarding the "infinite worth of every human being" than does the traditional legend. This particular celebration has been chosen from a number of other experiments of a somewhat similar nature since it was one of the most impressive in our own experience.

Recently a number of other churches have enlarged the meaning of Christmas in another quite different and valuable way. Instead of dramatizing exclusively the legendary story of the birth of Jesus, they have dramatized also, or portrayed in tableau form, the legends of two other equally miraculous births, those of Confucius and of Buddha. When these three legends are presented to children together so that they can be compared, and the reasons for their ancient origins are explained, the impression the children receive of their real significance is quite different from the impression given when but one legend is told as if it were wholly unique and true, in the sense most children conceive of truth. These three stories can be found simply retold in *From Long Ago and Many Lands*.[1]

Such revisions of traditional customs are encouraging. We hope, moreover, that the time will come when other even more radically different ways of celebrating the Christmas festival will be tried. As it is now, we who believe Jesus was human are missing an annual opportunity to revive the world's memories (as well as to correct mistaken impressions) of the truly great man who once lived and risked his life in his effort to revitalize religion. A man who was at least one of humanity's great religious originators and one of the most influential and profound ethical prophets.

Even a simple telling by some able leader of one memorable incident from the life of Jesus in a special service of worship, or the dramatization of such a story by one of the classes, during the Christmas holidays would have significance.

## Natural Dramatic Climaxes

If the members of one or more of the classes in the Church School have been imaginatively reliving the drama of Jesus' short life, possibly through the help of such a book as *Jesus: The Carpenter's Son*,[2] they may well be encouraged to lead in the preparation for the Christmas celebration by planning to dramatize one of the situations which he faced with perceptive compassion and courage.

In my own experience, I found that as the years passed the children's eagerness to create their own dramas out of the historical materials they were imaginatively living with in their classes increased, whether they were dealing with Moses, David, Akhenaten, the various creation stories, or with Jesus. No other type of activity seemed to supply the opportunities for so many varieties of personal contributions as did these programs. There were always responsibilities for everyone in the class. Nothing ever excelled the children's own dramatic programs in attracting the interest of parents and friends, and in contributing to their understanding of the nature of what was going on in our Church School. No other kind of service of worship called for the use of so many different forms of artistic expression in music, pictorial art, dancing, creative writing, acting, speaking, planning and making of scenery and costuming, and even mechanical skills. No other kind of activity seemed to elicit so much fresh imaginative thinking and feeling. No other kind of climax seemed to give the children themselves greater delight or deeper satisfaction.

## Let the Year's End Be a Climax

The second sample of a dramatic climaxing worship service that is illustrated here, is called "The Doorway from Past to Present." In this service each class chose two representatives to participate as characters. One was to become the personality from the past whom the class chose from among those whose lives they had been studying through the year. The other was to be a child of today who would talk with the historical character as if he were alive, having just stepped out of the doorway from the past into the present. This general plan required the children to compare and contrast the past and the present, a process that stimulated their imaginations and helped to make the ancient characters come alive. The doorway was constructed by several mechanically minded boys and made a simple dramatic symbol of the passing of time. Only the characters from the past needed costumes.

The entire program was both simple and impressive. The parents who came enjoyed the revelation they were given of the range of historical personalities the department had been studying. They enjoyed also the children's natural naive ways of expressing their thinking about the long ago and the now.

Both beginnings and endings call for some special celebrations of remembrance. A year's study without some expressed heartening culmination is like a story without a climax, a tree without fruit brought to ripeness. In the very nature of this living universe, every fulfilled living process is intended to become the seedling for a fresh beginning. Thus life goes on and on.

# Illustrations from Experience

## *A Dramatic Christmas Service of Worship: Every Babe a Miracle*

### The Story of Its Preparation

The idea for such a Christmas program began in a meeting of the Departmental Council which consisted of one representative from each class, plus one adult advisor. Next the teachers discussed the plan some six weeks before Christmas, and of course it was discussed in each separate classroom.

Several of the December services of worship were devoted to preparing all the children of the department to appreciate the symbolism to be embodied in the program. In one service, for example, we expressed the feelings and thoughts that come to us as we look at lighted candles.

At another gathering I told briefly the story of that famous astronomer of Denmark, Tycho Brahe, who lived when Galileo was alive. Being a man of some wealth, Brahe had built for his personal use a small observatory on his own estate. There, all by himself, he used to spend almost every clear night looking at the stars through his telescope and measuring their movements. For Tycho Brahe, to spend half the night watching the stars in the sky was like going to church. It was even more special, for he said he felt he was sitting alone in the presence of God. Because he felt this way, Tycho Brahe would always put on his very best suit of clothes before he went out to do his watching. "Why do you do this?" his friends would ask. "Because I feel that each night is a 'holy night.'"

We sang the carol "Silent Night! Holy Night!" and thought about Tycho Brahe as we sang it. The writer of that song thought of but one special night as being "holy night," but Brahe thought of every night as a "holy night." What did he mean? What would we mean if we said every day and every night are "holy"? People have called Jesus the "holy child." What might one mean who called every child a "holy child" or every birth night a "holy night"? So we wondered together. These meditations prepared us for feeling the meaning in our Christmas program.

Two of the classes chose to act the two family scenes. Fortunately, the woman who was helping us regularly with our dancing had recently given birth to a baby girl. Her husband and she, Mr. and Mrs. Kerry Smith, accepted our request that they be the parents in the family of today, and that their baby be the babe in the modern scene. As many members of the class as we could sensibly admit into the family became other children in the scene.

Each class regularly spent twenty minutes each Sunday in the gymnasium, where they danced their feelings and thoughts in some way or other. So another of the classes chose to be the dancers in the program. They talked over and worked out ways of dancing that would show how the influence of Jesus upon the world has been spreading like a light, growing slowly brighter and more outreaching with the years until it has spread into many lands all around the world. Such a dance they felt was the expression of a prayerful hope that someday the light of encouraging love might really spread among all mankind.

Although I have reported the actual words our children used in their dramatic conversations, it is hoped that no other group will simply reproduce these words. The emotional impressions produced by the two natural scenes were deep and moving because the children and adults were saying what *they had chosen to say* and not what someone else had given them to say.

Preparations for such cooperative dramatic ventures as this can be shortened and made less demanding if the adult leaders write the words and the children are given copies of what they are to say, and so need merely to be helped to say the words clearly and effectively. Such procedures, however, do not merely reduce the time and effort needed for preparing a production, they also usually reduce the rich, intangible inner values the children achieve when they know *that the product has been in large measure their own creation.*

## The Two Speaking Candles

A boy and a girl stood on either side of the stage in front of the large curtain throughout the acting of the two scenes. Each was dressed in a long, loose robe, and held a large candle in his right hand. Long hollow tubes of cardboard were used as holders for the short,

thick candles so that they seemed to be about three feet
tall. These two "Living Candles" announced the scenes
and interpreted them after they were acted.

Appropriate Christmas carols were sung by the
assembly before the acting began, and also between the
scenes and before the dancing.


### Scene 1. A Family of Today on Christmas Eve

[*The family feels under the spell of wondering at the
miracle of a newborn baby. Characters are Father,
Mother, Baby, and six other children. As the curtains
separate, a modern living room is suggested by a couch
and standing lamp on the right side, and by a single
upholstered chair on the left side, and a lighted,
trimmed Christmas tree on a small table near the center
at the back. As the curtains opened the Mother was
singing Isaac Watt's "Cradle Song."*]

> Hush my dear, lie still and slumber;
> Loving care surrounds thy bed.
> Heavenly blessings without number
> Gently fall upon thy head.
> Sleep, my babe; thy food and raiment,
> House and home, thy friends provide.
> All without thy care and payment,
> All thy wants are well supplied.

[*As the mother neared the end of the carol, the father
came and sat beside her on the couch. Father speaks as
the carol ends.*]

FATHER. Baby seems to have liked that carol as much
as I, though I hardly think she's very sleepy.

MOTHER. Why should she be? This is her first Christmas eve. No wonder she is excited.

FATHER. Just think, last Christmas she wasn't even here.

MOTHER. We could only imagine what she would be like. And now she's so much more wonderful than we could have hoped for.

FATHER. I suppose all parents share this feeling of wonder. Every baby is a miracle.

MOTHER. Next year she'll be toddling around on her two feet. And twenty Christmases from now, what will she be like then?

FATHER. I find it hard to picture her as a grown woman like you, the mother of a family!

MOTHER. Can you see these chubby little hands writing a letter or playing the piano?

FATHER. I wonder if her world will still be war-torn like ours?

MOTHER. And what will her part be in the building of peace on earth?

VIRGINIA [*Enters at this point and crosses over to the tree.*] Is it time to put our presents under the tree, Daddy?

FATHER. Just about time, my dear.

VIRGINIA. [*Crossing to right.*] Goody! It's time to bring our gifts! Daddy says so. (*Exits.*)

[*Father goes to the tree, and rearranges the lights.*]

VIRGINIA. [*Enters with gifts.*] Don't peek, Mother! I made this for you. [*Puts gifts on table under tree.*] The others are finishing their wrapping. [*Virginia puts a bit of tinsel on tree and walks slowly over to the baby and sits on the couch.*]

CAROL. [*Enters with Ronald.*] Do you think Baby will like this? It's a rattle. [*Places gift, touches balls on tree, goes to back of couch and looks at baby.*]

RONALD. I have a book for Uncle Ted. [*Looks at Carol.*] What are you giving, Carol?

CAROL. I'm giving Grandfather Edgerton an ashtray. I made it all by myself in craft class at school. Shut your eyes, Virginia. This is for you.

VIRGINIA. [*Hiding her eyes.*] All right. I won't peek.

MOTHER. I think our tree is more beautiful this year than ever.

FATHER. We all had a share in trimming it. Even little Bobby helped. He had to stand on a chair to reach the branches.

BRUCE. [*Enters with his little brother, Bobby, who is carrying a candy cane and holding on to Bruce.*] I have something for everybody! [*Places gifts on the tree. Goes to the large chair, sits down with Bobby.*]

CAROL. We forgot the star! Daddy, please put the star on top! [*Father places star on top of tree, while children gather about, add their finishing touches and pause to survey their work.*]

BRUCE. It looks swell, Dad.

VIRGINIA. [*Goes to tree, looks at gifts.*] There's a gift for everyone in our family and for some others, too. It's like having a birthday for *everybody,* all on one day!

MOTHER. A wonderful thought, Virginia. Christmas *is* everybody's birthday! [*Children group about mother to say good-night to the baby.*]

BRUCE. [*Goes with Bobby to Mother, sits on couch.*] Mother, does everybody in the world get a present on Christmas?

MOTHER. We wish it were true that everyone everywhere might be remembered by someone who loved him. That would be a great dream come true, something Jesus would have been happy to have seen happen.

FATHER. Then all the people of the world would really be like one great big family! [*The family sits quietly as the two candles speak.*]

CANDLE I.

And so the children come.
And so they have been coming.
Always in the same way they come—
Born of the seed of man and woman.
No angels herald the glory of their beginnings.
No prophets predict their future courses.
No wise men see a star that shows them where to
  find
The babe who will save mankind.

CANDLE II.

Yet each night a child is born is a holy night.
Fathers and mothers
Sitting beside their children's cribs
Feel glory in the wondrous sight of a new life
  beginning.
They ask, "Where and how will this new life
  end?"
"Or will it ever end?"
Each night a child is born is a holy night—
A time for singing,
A time for worshipping,
For heaven and earth are joined in the new
  creation.

[*The curtains are closed.*]

   *Interlude: The audience joins in singing "Joy to the World," adapted from words by Isaac Watts, 1719, by S. L. Fahs. Music by George Frederick Handel, 1742.*

Joy to the world where Love is come,
Let songs of gladness ring.
Let every heart cast off all gloom,
And Men and Nature sing!
And Men and Nature sing!

Joy to the world where Truth is said,
Where Trust and Knowledge guide.
Where slander's roots no longer spread,
And warm Goodwill is tried!
And warm Goodwill is tried!

No more let wars add wrong to wrong,
But friendly ways be found.
Not strong against the weak;
Nor weak against the strong,
But peace the wide world round!
But peace the wide world round!

## Scene 2. A Family in Nazareth Nearly Two Thousand Years Ago

   [*Characters are Father (Joseph), Mother (Mary), New-born Babe (Jesus). Scene is a simple peasant's cottage. A small bench stands to the right of a plain wooden crib. A brass bowl stands in the middle of the floor, a small fire burning in it.*
   *On a couple of shelves at back of room are some pieces of plain pottery. Parents are simply dressed in Hebrew costumes. Babe is wrapped in a tight-fitting*

*swaddling cloth, being held in his mother's arms. When curtains open, Mary, sitting on bench, is singing a lullaby. We used an old Hebrew melody and words. Father is bending over the fire.]*

MARY. Isn't he a lovely baby?

JOSEPH. And a real little fellow with a mind of his own!

MARY. Every day and all day long I thank God for him in my heart.

JOSEPH. He is truly a gift to us from God Most High. [*Father walks behind the bench.*]

MARY. And he will be like you, Joseph.

JOSEPH. Do you suppose he will be a carpenter? I will teach him. [*Father sits down beside mother.*]

MARY. Then he will be a good carpenter, Joseph. You will teach him to be a good one.

JOSEPH. And we will teach him the religion of our people. He must grow up to be a good man.

MARY. Yes, good like you, Joseph. Good to people who are poor and sick and troubled.

JOSEPH. Little son, do you know we are talking about you?

MARY. [*Fondling the baby.*] We'll be taking him to the temple in Jerusalem when he is a big boy.

JOSEPH. That will be a proud day for us. I remember well the trip I took to Jerusalem when I was twelve. But times are different now. The Romans would destroy our temple if they dared. It may not be there in twelve years.

MARY. Oh Joseph, they would not do that. Perhaps our baby will be a rabbi some day. He might even teach in the great temple.

JOSEPH. Or perhaps he will join the rebels against

the Romans and will lead us back into freedom again. Everyone is praying for someone to save us.

MARY. Those who lead rebellions get into trouble with the Romans. Sooner or later they are always caught and killed. Oh Joseph, let us teach our Jesus not to fight.

JOSEPH. But he must not be a coward, Mary. [*Father rises and speaks emphatically.*] These are dangerous times. We need men who are brave enough to fight against wrong. We must teach our boy to be true to the right even if he must die for it.

MARY. Yes, Joseph, we must teach him to be true to God's commandments. But let us teach him to be a carpenter, too. A good one like you, Joseph. Let him become known as an honest worker and a kind man respected by his neighbors.

JOSEPH. Which will it be, little son? [*Turning to baby.*] A carpenter, a rabbi, or a captain of armies? May God Almighty lead you! Let Him teach you His ways. May you keep His commandments. Then you will never need to fear what man can do to you.

MARY. I wish I could feel as brave as I want to be. Somehow I fear for this child. I feel that terrible things are going to happen and that he is going to suffer at the hands of cruel men. If only we could be sure that he would always do the right as he sees the right. Then he will be really great no matter what may happen to him. Behold us, thy servants, Oh God. Do unto us as it seems good to thee. [*Last two lines spoken as a prayer.*]

CANDLE 1. Father and mother of this child, whom you have named Jesus, if only you could come back to life again after these centuries, you would find that far more than you hoped for has come true of your son.

CANDLE II. You had hoped that perhaps he might in some way help to free your people from their cruel bondage to foreign rulers.

CANDLE I. Your son, Jesus, has done something greater than that. He has freed the minds of thousands of frightened and troubled people of many races.

CANDLE II. You had hoped that he might become a great rabbi, learned in the laws of Moses.

CANDLE I. Your son, Jesus, has become the greatest of the rabbis, a teacher whose words have been cherished and followed by thousands of people of all nations on earth, for nearly two thousand years.

CANDLE II. You had hoped that he might be brave and true to the truth as he saw it.

CANDLE I. Your son, Jesus, has become the very symbol of truth.

CANDLE II. You hoped that he would be kind and gentle to those who suffered.

CANDLE I. Your son, Jesus, because of his sympathy for those who were sick or blind or lame or despised has become our highest ideal of love itself, even of the great love of God.

CANDLE II. Your son, Jesus, has become like a great light shining in our darkness to lead us on to better ways of living.

CANDLE I. And the three of you, Joseph, Mary, and Jesus, we call you our Holy Family. Millions of families, scattered far and wide over the earth, have been blessed through you. May the circles of blessing grow wider and wider as the years pass by until the whole world becomes one great holy family bound together in peace and good will, worthy to be called children of God.

[*The curtains close.*]

*A Prayer Dance*

Presenting the hope of the spread of the light of love from small beginnings to many peoples. (Given by a fifth grade class.) The platform was bare except for an unlighted seven-branched candlestick on a pulpit in the back. A child stood at right front of stage and gave the running comment interpreting the dance that followed.

| *Running Comment* | *Dance Movements* |
|---|---|
| Our prayer shall now be given not only in words but also in a dance. | Piano plays continuously. |

*[Curtains open.]*

| | |
|---|---|
| There is a darkness within us when we feel lonely; when we become discouraged and afraid to try again; when we long for someone to care about us. Then our heads droop and our feet drag. | Dark stage.<br><br>Children sit slumped despondently or move slowly with bent backs and dragging feet. Some seem to be carrying burdens or doing tiring work. Each seems alone. |
| A friend comes to us. He understands how we feel. He helps us to try again. His confidence and love are like a bright light to us. He wakens us out of our gloom. He lights a | A child comes in with confident springing step. Goes to one in the group expressing friendliness and cheer. The stage becomes lighter. The child raises his head, appealed to by |

spark within us. Our hearts grow warm again. We can even be gay.

We feel uplifted and free. Our warmth kindles a light on the Tree of Life.

the warmth of his friend. He rises from the floor and enters into the skipping dance, sharing in the joy of companionship. The two go together to back of stage center and light the central candle of the seven-branched candelabra.

Now as a pair the two of us together go forth. We share in the work of others. We feel strong to relieve the overtired and discouraged. Gradually with our help they, too, are lifted to a free spirit. And now two more lights are kindled on the Tree of Life.

These two separate and each goes up to another despondent child. Soon the two pairs are dancing in a joyous skip.

These two pairs light the candles on either side of the central candle.

The two pairs become four pairs; and the four become eight. And so the lights multiply on the branches of the Tree of Life.

Then the two pairs seek four others. Then the eight join in the skipping dance. Then they all go to back of stage and light the remaining candles in the candelabra. In pairs the entire group perform a dance of joy that grows in strength. The pairs become quartets and then the entire group becomes one great semicircle, arms about each other's shoulders, facing the candelabra.

Something holy comes into being. A new love is born again and again. Out of fear comes courage. Out of darkness comes strength. Out of loneliness comes a togetherness. And so may the light continue, Ever growing, ever spreading. One heart answering to another—Mother to babe —Father to son—Friend to friend, friend to enemy —Never ending, ever growing, Ever spreading. Amen.

As these words are said, the dancers hold their positions in the semicircle.

Music continues to accompany the movements.

After the Amen is said, the music breaks into a swell as if of a growing radiance, and the children—each in his own place—turn around to face the audience. They raise their arms as if they were glowing flames of fire. Then

with their arms remaining
uplifted, and with joyous
expressions on their faces,
they move forward down
through the three aisles of
the audience room, carry-
ing the radiance of their
mood to the very back of
the room as a symbol of
the growth of love in life.

The service was then closed with a benediction
spoken by Dr. Ivar Hellstrom, the Minister of Education.

### A Dramatic Climax To A Year's Work

Preparatory Planning and Cooperation

This service originated in the discussions of the
Junior Department Council at Riverside Church in
New York City. Their ideas were reconsidered by the
teaching staff, and a slight revision was made which
finally resulted in the plan as reported.

Each class chose two of its members to take part,
one to represent a character from the past about whom
the class had studied, and the other a child from the
present. Only the characters from the past were in costume. An open doorway had been set up on the platform between two parts of the large curtain. It was
marked in large letters: "DOORWAY FROM THE
PAST."

As each character from the past in turn stepped out
through this doorway, he was met by a child of the

present who came forward from the front row of seats.
The two then conversed. At the close of the conversation the two joined hands and walked down from the
platform and sat down in the front row. The conversations in each instance were worked out by committees
representing the classes involved.

The initial call to meditation was written by the
departmental coordinator. Some sort of poetic, dignified and meaningful introduction to the pageant of
characters from the past seemed to be needed to give
the whole picture an appropriate setting.

### The Pageant: Through the Doorway
### From Past to Present

*Opening Song—Presenting the Theme
of the Service*

Now praise we good and noble men,
Forgotten ones and famous.
They blessed the world. Let them be blessed
For all the hope they gave us.
Praise we the wise and brave and strong,
Who graced their generations:
Who helped the right but not the wrong,
And bettered our relations.

Praise we the great of heart and mind,
The singers sweetly gifted,
Whose music wondrously designed,
Has weary folk uplifted.
Praise we the peaceful men of skill
Who builded homes of beauty,
And, rich in heart, made richer still
The brotherhood of duty.

Praise we those men who searched for truth,
Beyond the ancient learning.
Who spoke their thoughts sincerely forth,
Imprisoned—falsehood spurning.
Praise we the courage of their minds,
Who broke outworn traditions,
Who showed new truths for all mankind,
And bettered our condition.

[*Adapted from words by William George Tarrant. Third Stanza by S. L. Fahs. Tune: "Ellacombe" Hymn* 335 *in* American Student Hymnal, *by permission Fleming H. Revell Company.*]

*A Call to Thoughtfulness* (Spoken by the Leader)

Today our imaginations will take flight.
They will fly backward through centuries of time.
They will fly more swiftly than airplanes through the air.
Centuries will change into days,
and days will turn into minutes
till the long ago becomes now,
and the distant past stands within today.

Great heroes whose voices have long been silent
will awake to life.
They will fly forward through centuries of time—
to meet us at—The Great Doorway—
that divides today from all the yesterdays that have gone by.
These men of old will speak to us
and we shall talk with them;
for we shall all live together in the land of the spirit,
where time is forgotten,
where the dead still live,
where the living dream new dreams.

[*The doorway opens.*]

## I. AN AFRICAN BUSHMAN

AFRICAN BUSHMAN. I am a Primitive Man. I step out of the past to talk with you, my human descendant. Twenty-five thousand years ago I lived here on this earth. My home was a cave and I ran to it for safety. When the weather was good I lived in plenty and ate well. When droughts came the land was bare and times were hard. Often we would have to travel for miles to get even water to drink. Our children would cry because they were hungry and often we had no food for them and many of them died for that reason. But who are you?

CHILD OF TODAY. I am a girl of today. I live in an apartment in New York City. We do not go out and hunt for our food now. We buy it at the grocery store. We have other troubles, though not all the same as yours just as real for us: war, taxes, criminals, fires, and poverty. These may seem very strange to you, but they are problems for us.

AFRICAN BUSHMAN. When it came night we danced around our fires as a prayer to keep the wild animals and the witches away. Often we could hear noises of owls and jackals. Some of these we believed were trying to say things to us. We told many stories at night around our fires. In some of these we tried to tell of our wonderings about life then, and about death that we knew would come to us.

CHILD OF TODAY. Today we think of life and death, too. Now we have many hospitals, churches, and other institutions to help people who are sick or who need special help in other ways. We know that new babies are born and people die and still we cannot really understand either life or death. Perhaps we know no more than you did about death.

AFRICAN BUSHMAN. The trees and the flowers that grew around our caves caused us to wonder. Each winter we saw them die and leave the earth. Each spring they lifted new green foliage above the ground. "Surely," we said, "there must be some great power which we could never explain," but we had ideas about it.

CHILD OF TODAY. We, too, see new life appear in the spring and fade away with the winter. But we do not know the answer to this.

AFRICAN BUSHMAN. Like the death of the flowers and trees and other growing things around us we thought we might die and return again to the living. We could not say how this could be. We told stories, also, of the animals that we thought might help us.

CHILD OF TODAY. Now scientists are studying ruins of ancient peoples to help us understand the past better, and so that the future may be more understandable. They are studying medicine, astronomy, and many other great problems. Slowly man climbs through the long ages toward a better world. By understanding evolution we know better of man's struggle during life, but we are wondering all the time about what happens after life. Surely there is more wonder to come than we can think of now.

## II. JOSEPH

CHILD OF TODAY. How do you do. Can I help you? You seem to be a stranger here.

JOSEPH. I am a stranger. I have come back after 3,000 years to see what progress has been made on the earth.

CHILD OF TODAY. Your costume reminds me of the ancient Hebrews whom we have been studying this year. Could you, by chance, be Joseph?

JOSEPH. I am that Joseph who was sold by his brothers and who became governor of Egypt.

CHILD OF TODAY. I am very glad to welcome you. We have many questions we would like to ask you. Have you looked about our city?

JOSEPH. I have just arrived, but on my way here I saw many things which astonished me. What were those carriages and heavy wagons which moved without horses or men to draw them?

CHILD OF TODAY. Those are automobiles. About one hundred fifty years ago man learned how to use a great force in nature which he calls power. Man has made machines driven by this power which do much of his hard work today.

JOSEPH. This is a wonderful thing. I remember the cruel, terrible, hard labor that slaves endured in Egypt. Now you must be able to raise enough food for everybody.

CHILD OF TODAY. Some people tell us today that enough food, homes, and clothing could be produced for everyone, but poverty is still very great.

JOSEPH. Why do you not use this great power you say man has discovered to raise food and to make things people need?

CHILD OF TODAY. You have asked a hard question. Many people ask that question. But if you think things seem bad in our country you would find them worse in other parts of the world.

JOSEPH. What is happening there?

CHILD OF TODAY. Terrible wars are being fought on

three continents. Nations are using this great power to make war-machines to destroy one another.

JOSEPH. That sounds as though man had lost his mind.

CHILD OF TODAY. Can you tell us anything we might do about it?

JOSEPH. Do you suppose that if, when you quarrelled or were unkind or unfair to one another, you made up instead of letting hate grow, it would help?

CHILD OF TODAY. That is hard to do. When we quarrel we each think we are right. But you are Joseph. You forgave when your brothers had treated you cruelly. Did you find it hard to forgive?

JOSEPH. When my brothers came to Egypt it was twenty years after they sold me. The hard things which had happened to me had made me think. I saw that I was partly to blame. When I saw that my brothers really loved Benjamin and my father, it was not hard to forgive them.

CHILD OF TODAY. You say you saw that you were partly to blame. Did you find it hard to admit you were wrong and not blame all your troubles on your brothers?

JOSEPH. I was such a spoiled child I could think of no one but myself for a long time. But the hard work I had to do was good for me. After a time I began to think more honestly.

CHILD OF TODAY. Do you think that if we learned to think more honestly we could forgive more easily? Is it important for us to learn to forgive?

JOSEPH. Everyone needs to forgive and be forgiven many times during his life. These things are hard. Do not be discouraged but keep on trying. To learn to be honest and fair and forgiving, this will take you a lifetime. Does it seem worthwhile?

CHILD OF TODAY. We thank you, Joseph, for encouraging us. Whenever we read your life story in the Bible we shall remember that you did not let the hard things you had to face spoil your life.

## III. AKHENATEN

AKHENATEN. Good morning to you, young fellow. Do you live in this part of the country?

CHILD OF TODAY. Yes, I live very near. But you must have come from far away. You are like the pictures I have seen of people who lived long ago. Who are you?

AKHENATEN. I am Akhenaten. Three thousand years ago I lived in Egypt, on the River Nile, as Pharaoh of Upper and Lower Egypt.

CHILD OF TODAY. Oh yes, I studied about you. I remember some interesting things that you did when you were Pharaoh of Egypt.

AKHENATEN. I've come back to find out what people have been doing these past three thousand years. Is this tall building your temple?

CHILD OF TODAY. Yes, we call it our church.

AKHENATEN. Your church is as high as our pyramids. It is very beautiful. Are all churches today like this one?

CHILD OF TODAY. No, this is one of the largest. We do interesting things here besides worship. Many grown people and children come here every day in the week to work and to play together in a friendly way.

AKHENATEN. That is very fine. A few minutes ago I saw from the window a giant thunder bird flying across the sky. Have you a name for it? Is it a new god?

CHILD OF TODAY. That is an airplane, a machine that flies. Man made that. It isn't a god.

AKHENATEN. Why did man make such a thing?

CHILD OF TODAY. The first airplanes were made for people to travel in, but right now they are used more for fighting in the war.

AKHENATEN. War! What war?

CHILD OF TODAY. The World War. Most of the countries in the world are at war.

AKHENATEN. Why are all these people fighting?

CHILD OF TODAY. People today don't want war any more than you wanted it long ago, but one unfriendly act brings another unfriendly act, and so war spreads and spreads like a terrible fire. Thousands of these airplanes are fighting night and day, destroying cities and killing many people by dropping big bombs on them.

AKHENATEN. Airplanes, bombs, war! What a terrible waste. I thought those savage days of war in our times were over. No good can come of all this destruction. Haven't people learned that war is useless in all these three thousand years? I tried very hard to help my people believe that war was useless. I hoped when I died that they would spread my teaching to all the world. I just cannot believe it. After all these years, after all these years—most of the world is fighting.

CHILD OF TODAY. Yes, it is terrible and useless. It is worse today than it has ever been before.

AKHENATEN. Do these people who are fighting have any religion? Do they worship Aten or do they have many gods?

CHILD OF TODAY. Yes, our people have a religion. We worship and we pray, but we use the name *God*, not Aten, as you did. We have one God over all. You

were the very first leader who believed in only one God.
I remember reading that.

AKHENATEN. Then we do believe the same and
think alike in some ways. For this we give thanks to
the God of all people. May he help people today to
understand that one unfriendly act brings another unfriendly act and that no good can ever come of it.

## IV. MOSES

CHILD OF TODAY. Who are you?

MOSES. I am Moses. I lived in the early ages when
my people, the Hebrews, were slaves to the Egyptian
Pharaoh. They were made to haul heavy stones and
to make bricks of clay under the heat of the burning
sun.

CHILD OF TODAY. And what happened to these slaves,
Moses?

MOSES. I thought it was cruel that my people had
to undergo such hardships. I decided that in some way
I must free them.

CHILD OF TODAY. That was a great task, Moses.
How did you ever find a way of doing it?

MOSES. After a great deal of trouble had come to
the Egyptians, Pharaoh finally let my people go out
into the desert to worship our God Yahweh. Thus we
were able to escape over the Red Sea into the wilderness.

CHILD OF TODAY. Moses, no wonder your name has
come down to us through these centuries.

MOSES. Have there been any slaves since my time?

CHILD OF TODAY. Yes, Moses, and today we are
ashamed to admit that a great dictator has enslaved
many of the meek and defenseless people of the earth.

Tears and blood are being shed over many parts of the world. We do indeed have slaves today.

MOSES. I had no idea that the world would *ever* witness in the future what happened to my people in the past.

CHILD OF TODAY. Tell me, Moses, how did those freed slaves become a great people?

MOSES. It was hard to learn how to live as free people. There was fighting and quarrelling and stealing. We had to make rules to live by. The old laws talked about killing a man who injured you. We made a new rule: an eye for an eye and a tooth for a tooth. But today you don't live by *that* rule, do you?

CHILD OF TODAY. We wish we could say we lived differently. Jesus, who lived many years after you, taught us to love our enemies and to do good to them that hate us.

MOSES. That is a very *hard* teaching to live by, but a very wonderful teaching. Why doesn't the world follow it?

CHILD OF TODAY. People try to, and then they forget about it. They just think about themselves and about fighting back and getting even.

MOSES. Perhaps the people of the world today who have learned how to make it such a good place to live in, in so many ways, will also learn to live with one another in peace and happiness.

## V. SAMSON

SAMSON. What time is it? Who am I? I thought I was Samson.

CHILD OF TODAY. You've been asleep a long time,

nearly three thousand years. Since you went to sleep the Continent of America has been discovered.

SAMSON. What is happning to my people now? Have they conquered the Philistines? Are they treated well?

CHILD OF TODAY. Your people are scattered all over the world. In Germany and other countries they are being persecuted. All the fighting that you did during your lifetime has done little good for your people.

SAMSON. Are my people still fighting for their freedom?

CHILD OF TODAY. Your people are still fighting for freedom but have not succeeded in their cause because they are not powerful enough. There is another people that wants to conquer the world now. Hitler is their dictator. He is the cause of the great war we are having now.

SAMSON. Do people still have the same customs of religion? You remember I thought it was wrong to cut my hair, and I never drank wine. Are there people like that today?

CHILD OF TODAY. There are a few people that follow those customs.

SAMSON. Are there people today as strong as I was?

CHILD OF TODAY. There are people almost as strong as you. We can do even greater things than you did. We can tear down big buildings, but we do not do it with our arms. We do it with machines and bombs and dynamite.

SAMSON. A while ago I heard a noise up in the air. What was it?

CHILD OF TODAY. It was an airplane that carries passengers through the air. That is a way of travelling fast. It is good. Sometimes people's lives are saved that way.

But airplanes sometimes are used in another way, to destroy people's buildings and homes and hospitals and many other things.

SAMSON. I see that you still waste your powers the way I did. I should think you would have learned better after three thousand years.

## VI. SAINT AUGUSTINE

SAINT AUGUSTINE. I shall come forth and praise the Christian Way of Living.

CHILD OF TODAY. Saint Augustine, how did you happen to think of the Story of Salvation?

SAINT AUGUSTINE. I found it in the Bible, and I put together the ideas of salvation that I found there. I wanted to make it possible for all people to go to heaven.

CHILD OF TODAY. Where do you believe heaven is?

SAINT AUGUSTINE. Heaven is in the sky above the clouds. God sits there on a golden throne with Jesus at his right hand.

CHILD OF TODAY. I don't see just how that could be. Our scientists tell us that the universe is of great extent, made up of stars and planets whirling in order. We do not think that God is in just one place.

SAINT AUGUSTINE. Where do you think God is, then?

CHILD OF TODAY. I think there is a little bit of God in the heart of every living thing. Even the plants could not live without a Creator. God protects all creatures by natural camouflage, because God is in nature.

SAINT AUGUSTINE. That does not sound like my story.

CHILD OF TODAY. The scientists have found out many things about evolution.

SAINT AUGUSTINE. What is evolution?

CHILD OF TODAY. Evolution is the process of all living things growing, developing, and changing through the ages. All of life comes in the first place from one tiny cell and develops into great living things. And in the process, all of life comes from God.

SAINT AUGUSTINE. I thought that men at my time knew the answers to all of their questions.

CHILD OF TODAY. We are still learning and finding out new things. We are learning more all the time about science, about evolution, and about God. We are even beginning to feel differently about God.

SAINT AUGUSTINE. How do you feel differently about God?

CHILD OF TODAY. We do not believe that God is way off somewhere. We feel that God is with us all the time, working in and through all people.

SAINT AUGUSTINE. Well, I think I can see your point of view. In a changing world such as you spoke of, man has to change his ideas about many things, even about God.

## VII. GALILEO

GALILEO. Where am I? [*Rubbing his eyes.*] And who are you? [*Looking up.*]

CHILD OF TODAY. I'm Joan Grote. I live in America. But what funny clothes you have on! You look like somebody I've seen in a picture book of people of long ago.

GALILEO. I'm Galileo—a poor scientist.

CHILD OF TODAY. Galileo! Oh, how wonderful! How did you get here? I thought you were dead over three hundred years ago.

GALILEO. I don't know how I got here. I must have been asleep for a long time. What's been happening in the world since I died? Do people still think that the world is flat and that the sun goes around it?

CHILD OF TODAY. Oh no, Galileo, everybody thinks now that the earth is round and that it moves around the sun as you used to say.

GALILEO. I'm so happy to hear this! I tried to show my students and the Pope that they were wrong, but they would not listen. They were afraid. They thought that they would lose their religion if they did not believe that the earth was the center of everything. Do people still believe in God, and do they have churches where they go to worship?

CHILD OF TODAY. Yes, indeed, Galileo. You are in a church now. The more we learn the more wonderful the universe seems to be. We think there must be a God who planned it all.

GALILEO. You make me feel happy, little girl. Tell me, do people still look through telescopes?

CHILD OF TODAY. Oh yes, Galileo. We have many telescopes now. We have them on ships and on airplanes. We have a huge one on top of one of our mountains.

GALILEO. And do people look at the stars through these telescopes?

CHILD OF TODAY. Oh yes, Galileo.

GALILEO. And have you found out anything more about the stars?

CHILD OF TODAY. We keep finding out new things all the time, Galileo. We think there are millions of stars and some of them are much bigger than our sun.

GALILEO. I'm so glad I could come alive again. Tell me more, little girl. Do people still use microscopes?

CHILD OF TODAY. Yes, indeed, Galileo. We use microscopes a great deal now. We can make them now so that they will magnify a thing more than a *thousand times!*

GALILEO. And what can people see through these microscopes?

CHILD OF TODAY. Doctors use them all the time. They have found so many, many things about our bodies you never dreamed of, Galileo. Why, they know now that a great many kinds of sickness are caused by tiny little germs that get into the blood.

GALILEO. Germs? What are they?

CHILD OF TODAY. They are the tiniest living things you can imagine. Some of them do us a lot of harm.

GALILEO. You make me feel very small, like a child just beginning to learn.

CHILD OF TODAY. But we think you were very important, Galileo. And we are so glad you did not let those Inquisitors burn your books. They have been read by thousands of people. Because of what you did people began to experiment, and so men really began to learn. And now you are greatly respected everywhere. We thank God that you lived.

The service was closed by all joining in reading a responsive reading that was the result of discussions in the several classes. The reading was put together by Mrs. Edwards. In closing we sang, "Our God Our Help in Ages Past."

[*This service was given at Riverside Church, New York City, May 10, 1940.*]

# Notes

**Chapter One:**

1. Ralph W. Emerson, "The Divinity School Address," in *Three Prophets of the Liberal Faith*. Boston: Beacon Press, 1961. Beacon LR 12.
2. Arnold Toynbee, "New Vistas for the Historian." *Saturday Review,* January 7, 1956.

**Chapter Two:**

1. Lin Yu-tang, *My Country and My People*. New York: Reynal and Hitchcock, 1935, p. 13.
2. Christmas Humphreys, *Zen Buddhism*. New York: Macmillan Co., and London: William Heinemann, 1949.

**Chapter Three:**

1. James Martineau, "Ideal Substitutes for God." American Unitarian Association. Out of print.
2. John Baillie, *Our Knowledge of God*. New York: Scribner's Sons, 1939, pp. 55-57.
3. Edmund W. Sinnott, *The Biology of the Spirit*. New York: Viking Press, 1955.
4. Weston La Barre, *The Human Animal*. Chicago: University of Chicago Press, 1955.
5. Loren Eiseley, *The Immense Journey*. New York: Random House, 1957.
6. Fred G. Bratton, *The First Heretic*. Boston: The Beacon Press, 1962.

**Chapter Four:**

1. Robert T. Weston, from a sermon privately printed in a booklet, "Seven Sunday Mornings," issued by the First Unitarian Church of Louisville, Kentucky.
2. Archibald MacLeish, "The Hamlet of A. MacLeish," *Collected Poems*. Boston: Houghton Mifflin Company, 1963, p. 219.
3. Ralph W. Emerson, *Emerson's Essays: First Series*. Boston: Houghton Mifflin, (Riverside Library).

4. Sophia L. Fahs, and Dorothy T. Spoerl, *Beginnings: Earth, Sky, Life, Death*. Revised edition. Boston, The Beacon Press, 1960.

5. Personal letter from Albert Einstein to Phyllis Wright. Translated from the German.

Chapter Five:

1. Walt Whitman, *Leaves of Grass*. Poem, "Starting from Paumanok." New York: David McKay, 1900.

2. Vladimir Lundenberg, *Meditation and Mankind*. Translated from the German by Betty Collins. London: Rider and Co. Ltd., 1950, p. 27.

Chapter Six:

1. Carl J. Nelson, *Eternity Can Wait*. Milford, New Hampshire: The Hunter Press, 1962, page 172.

2. R. R. Marrett, *Faith, Hope and Charity in Primitive Religion*. New York: The Macmillan Co., 1952.

3. Herbert Kuhn, *On the Track of Pre-Historic Man*. New York: Random House, 1955.

Chapter Seven:

1. Sophia L. Fahs, *From Long Ago and Many Lands*. Boston: The Beacon Press, 1948.

2. Sophia L. Fahs, *Jesus: The Carpenter's Son*. Boston: The Beacon Press, 1945.